Bible WORDS
and Theological Terms
MADE EASY
a practical handbook

Wayne Jackson

Bible Words and Theological Terms Made Easy - A Practical Handbook

©2002 by Courier Publications

All rights reserved. No part of this book may be reproduced in any form without written permission of the publisher except in the case of brief quotations embodied in critical articles or reviews.

ISBN 0-9678044-6-9

Additional copies may be ordered from:

Courier Publications
7809 N. Pershing Ave.
Stockton, CA 95207

http://www.christiancourier.com
http://www.courierpublications.com

FOREWORD

Of all the biological creatures upon the earth, only human beings understand words as "symbols" of ideas. A dog may be conditioned to "sit" upon command. Though he responds to the "signal," he does not really comprehend what it means to "sit" (as opposed to standing), nor does he fathom any rationale as to why the command is given. Adam's descendants are different. God has "spoken" (Heb. 1:1) to mankind, and he has done so in "words."

Words constitute the vehicles of thought. They convey volumes of meaningful information, and every person, who is cognizant of the value of his own mind, ought to be a student of words. The message of human redemption is framed in words, and without an understanding of a certain level of those words, one cannot be saved from his sins (cf. Acts 11:14).

It is said that the Old Testament contains some 8,600 Hebrew and Aramaic words, while the New Testament has about 5,600 Greek terms. One could spend a lifetime studying biblical words and never exhaust the thrilling endeavor. This little book is about words. It is, for the most part, about *Bible* words – what certain terms mean, and how they are used within respective contexts of sacred scripture.

Words From God

Over the past twenty centuries, various views have been entertained regarding the nature of the Bible. Some have held it to be an interesting, even classical piece of ancient literature, but certainly not of heavenly origin with the mandate of divine authority.

On the other hand, multiplied thousands, who have carefully explored the pages of the timeless Book, have been driven to the conclusion that the Scriptures are far more than a mere human production. The revered volume has a distinctly supernatural character.

Actually, that is precisely what the writers of the biblical documents claimed. They humbly acknowledged that the works they were producing did not originate with them; rather, the ultimate Source was the Lord of heaven and earth. David wrote: "The Spirit of Jehovah spoke by me, and his word was upon my tongue" (2 Sam. 23:2).

The evidence that supports the biblical claim of sacred origin is staggering, and it manifests itself to the conscientious student in a variety of ways. One has only to consider the following categories to be amazed at the composition of the holy oracles.

Textual Evidence

For example, the sixty-six documents that compose the Book are characterized by a marvelous flow of continuity. There is such an amazing harmony of the narratives, that it is impossible that they could have been authored over a span of sixteen centuries, by some forty writers, and then, have flowed together fortuitously in the fashion now found. The Bible's unity argues for a supreme, orchestrating Mind.

Additionally, there are approximately 1,000 prophecies that adorn the pages of this body of literature. The fact that these fore-statements (dealing with nations, people, events, etc.) were fulfilled perfectly is more than incredible. One need only consider the some 300 prophecies that precisely prophesied the Savior's mission to be awed by the divine foreknowledge that is a part of the biblical package.

One is forced to marvel at the uncanny accuracy of the Scriptures in the different academic areas upon which they touch – whether it is history, science, geography, etc. We have discussed this matter in detail in our book, *The Bible & Science*.

Baffling Omissions

But there are other lines of evidence that add weight to the biblical claim of supernatural origin. Some of these are more indirect in nature. For example, there are omissions in the Bible that are puzzling had its composition been directed by mere human impulse. Why are there no descriptions of God, or of Jesus Christ? Other volumes of religious literature abound with portrayals of the features of their divine characters.

Why were most of the biographical data of Jesus' thirty-three years upon this earth passed over in silence? Why do we know almost nothing of the life-long labors of most of the apostles? Writers guided by their own literary inclinations would scarcely have neglected such intriguing information. This is not a circumstance easily explained from a naturalistic point of view. Elsewhere we have dealt with this matter in more detail. See our web site (http://www.christiancourier.com - **Archives**, "The Scriptures' Silence – An Argument For Inspiration," February 8, 1999.

Strange Inclusions

If a writer is attempting to perpetrate a religious hoax by means of bogus documents, he will make every effort to avoid controversial issues which would "turn off" those he hopes to persuade by his propaganda. In view of this well-recognized principle, one is shocked to note some very strange inclusions to the New Testament record – if the narratives were prepared by writers who knew Christianity to be a contrived system, yet, nonetheless, wanted to persuade first-century citizens to accept it. Consider some of the following cases.

If fabricated, the narratives regarding Jesus' birth would hardly have been begun with the story of an out-of-wedlock birth – a most disgraceful circumstance in the first century. Would a publican, like Matthew, have been selected to write a Gospel account designed to appeal to the Jews – when the Jews despised publicans (tax collectors employed by the pagan Romans)? Since Hebrew men disdained all public association with women, would Christ have been portrayed as a friend of women – had a forger been attempting to construct an admirable image? Would a fabricator have made heroes of "Samaritans," as Luke's gospel did on more than one occasion? These strange "inclusions" reveal a sense of genuineness.

In summarizing these major points we may say: (a) There are things *in* the Bible that *could not* have been the result of mere human intellect. (b) There are things *not in* the Bible that surely *would have been there* if the documents had been humanly engineered. (c) There are incidents recorded in the Bible that *would not have been placed there* if mere human impulse had been the guiding force in its composition.

The Words of the Bible

Granted, then, that the Bible is, in some sense, a revelation from God. To what *extent* did divine "inspiration" (cf. 2 Tim. 3:16-17) characterize the original documents?

Some, who profess a friendship with the Scriptures, allege

that the writings are "inspired" in "sense" only, but not in "sentence." In other words, though the "thoughts" may be heavenly, the phraseology was strictly human, and one cannot be confident, therefore, that the message is *without error.* Actually, this concept makes little sense. One might as well speak of a "tune" without "notes," as to talk of "thoughts" in the absence of "words." The truth of the matter is, the Scriptures are permeated with the affirmation that, ultimately, its writers were guided by the Spirit of God in the very *words* they chose (see Mt. 10:19; Lk. 21:12-17), even though their respective personalities are reflected in the vocabulary they employed.

Jesus once declared that man must direct his life by the "words" that proceed from God (Mt. 4:4). If those "words" are not to be found in the Bible, where, pray tell, are they? The very term "Scripture" denotes a *writing*, and the biblical "writings" consist of units of "words." Inasmuch, then, as "every scripture" is said to be "inspired of God" (2 Tim. 3:16), the clear conclusion must be that the biblical words themselves are inspired.

The study of Bible words is one of the most exciting adventures in which one can engage. Words may be investigated from a variety of vantage points. The etymology of a word (i.e., its original stem, along with prefixes or suffixes that may be appended) may be revealing. A term's special use, e.g., its relationship to other words within a phrase or a sentence, can be crucial to the correct interpretation of a passage. Is a particular word a verb, a noun, an adjective, a preposition, etc.? A term's grammatical information can help to illuminate; for example, is the verb active or passive in its "voice"? Does it suggest a question or statement by its "mood"? Is it a past, present, or future form, in terms of its time element? These are vital aspects the serious student must explore.

Bible Words and Theological Terms Made Easy

Of special importance in studying Bible words is the context in which a term is found. Context is everything! The contextual significance of a term can override all other considerations. Studying the text of the sacred Scriptures is a challenge indeed, but one that yields the most delightful rewards.

Theological Words

In addition to biblical words, this volume deals with some words that have been formed to express certain religious doctrines and/or ideas. These are terms not found in the biblical text, but they are used in religious contexts to express significant ideas. Sometimes they are called "theological" terms. They pertain, in some way or another, to things within the realm of the sacred.

This volume has not been designed for scholars who have the ability, the time, and the resources to consult compositions that are much more erudite than this abbreviated effort. This book is intended for the average Christian student, the new convert, the Bible class teacher, or even the busy minister, who, on occasion, may need to utilize a quick reference source.

It is the author's hope that this "practical handbook" will provide a beneficial service to sincere students of Scripture in our rapidly-paced world of changing communication outlets.

> *Words are things;*
> *and a small drop of ink,*
> *falling like dew upon a thought,*
> *produces that which makes thousands,*
> *perhaps millions, think.*
>
> *Lord Byron*

ABOMINATION

The English Bible uses the word "abomination" to reflect about a dozen terms in the original languages of both Testaments. The prevailing idea behind the words is that of a divine revulsion at transgressions pertaining to religious and moral matters. The various words are employed in different senses, and sometimes reflect degrees of displeasure. (a) Idols and the worship thereof was an abomination unto God (Isa. 66:3; Jer. 4:1; 2 Kgs. 16:3). (b) Worship offered to God, if done with the wrong spirit, also is abominable (Prov. 15:8; Isa. 1:13). (c) Sexual sins, e.g., homosexuality, is an abomination before God (Lev. 18:22). (d) Dishonorable treatment of one's fellows was characterized similarly (Prov. 12:22; 20:23). Note carefully the list of abominations catalogued in Proverbs 6:16ff. Those who yield themselves to the practice of abominable actions will not be permitted into heaven (Rev. 21:27).

ABOMINATION OF DESOLATION

This phrase has roots in the Old Testament. There are allusions to "the abomination that makes desolate" in the book of Daniel (cf. 9:27; 11:31; 12:11). It is generally believed that 11:31 is a reference to the *abominable* (evil) power that *desolated* the Jewish system during that historical period between the Testaments, particularly the reign of the Seleucid ruler, Antiochus Epiphanes (c. 175-63 B.C.). That heathen official viciously persecuted the Jews, attempted to destroy the Scriptures, and desecrated the temple. The reference in 9:27 clearly is to the destruction of Jerusalem in A.D. 70, when the idolatrous Romans crushed the Jewish regime, and Judaism, as a religious system, came to an end – and that by divine design (Mt. 22:7). This is the interpretation given the passage by the Lord himself (Mt. 24:15; Mk. 13:14; Lk. 21:20). The significance of the expression in Daniel 12:11 is more difficult. Some see it as a descriptive of Antiochus' persecution, while others view it as a reference to the destruction of Jerusalem, and the end of the Jewish sacrificial system. It may be that Antiochus' onslaught prefigured the desolation that the Romans would bring ultimately. The notion that it refers to a terrorizing "Antichrist" who will wreak havoc upon the people of God near the end of time, preceding an earthly reign of Christ, is without scriptural justification.

ABRAHAM'S BOSOM

It was the Jewish custom to "recline" at the table during meals in the first century. The saying, "recline in the bosom," signified a place of honor, such as the apostle John enjoyed at the Passover supper the night before Christ was crucified (cf. Jn. 13:23). The phrase is used of Jesus' intimate relationship with his Heavenly Father (Jn. 1:18). In Luke 16:23 the expression is employed to describe the state of blessedness afforded the beggar, Lazarus, following his death. The term not only reflects a *reward*, but also a place of *honor*; hence, it implies consciousness. It represents the condition of the godly soul between the time the body dies and the final resurrection of the same. It would be the equivalent of "paradise" (Lk. 23:43).

ACCURSED

The word "accursed" (KJV) translates the Greek *anathema* four times in the New Testament. It carries the idea of "devoted to destruction." (a) In Romans 9:3, Paul, by the use of a figure known as hyperbole (an exaggeration to emphasize), states he was at the point of wishing he might be cut off from Christ, if such could somehow have effected salvation for the Jews. The statement is a commentary on the apostle's tremendous love for his people. (b) Elsewhere, Paul contends that no one, speaking by the guidance of the Holy Spirit, could declare Jesus "accursed" (1 Cor. 12:3). The meaning of "accursed" here may be – "deserving of death." This may reflect a charge being made about Christ by some in that day. (c) Those who mingle the gospel of Christ with false doctrines will be eternally cut off from communion with God – if they continue in such a godless course (Gal. 1:8-9). (d) Anyone who refuses to "love the Lord," i.e., submit to his will in order to secure salvation (Jn. 14:15), is destined to be banished from God's presence, hence devoted to destruction (1 Cor. 16:22).

ACTS, BOOK OF

This book, written by Luke, was addressed to Theophilus, a Gentile Christian official. The aim of the narrative is to record the establishment of the church of Christ on the day of Pentecost (see reference), and the spread of the Christian movement throughout the ancient world – all the way to Rome. The book embodies some thirty-three years of Christian history. The first division of the book (chapters 1-12) deals principally with Peter's ministry among the Jews. The final portion (13-28), details Paul's labor among the Gentiles. The book records numerous examples of how men and women became Christians under the oversight of inspired apostles.

ADOPTION

The Greek word is *huiothesia*, from *huios*, "son," and *tithemi*, "to set, put, or place." The word suggests the idea of placing one into the position of a son. The term is found five times in the New Testament. (a) The Christian's reception of the Holy Spirit (see Acts 2:38) is God's pledge that he has been "adopted" as a son. Unlike Christ, who was "son" as to his very nature, i.e., deity (Heb. 5:8), we, by the new birth process (Jn. 3:3-5), have been adopted into the family of God (cf. Gal. 4:5; Eph. 1:5). (b) The future resurrection of the body at the last day is spoken of as an "adoption" (Rom. 8:23). This suggests there is a fuller measure of the "inheritance" than what we presently enjoy. (c) The nation of Israel experienced an "adoption" in the sense it was selected and used as a divine instrument to facilitate the coming of the Messiah (Rom. 9:4). Each individual Jew is accountable to God for his own *personal* obedience, of course (Rom. 1:16-17).

ADULTERY

Adultery is sexual intimacy between a married person and someone other than his/her lawful mate. The act begins in the mind (Mt. 5:28; Mk. 7:21) and ultimately manifests itself in a physical union (cf. Jn. 8:4). Adultery may be a casual "fling," or it may involve a relationship under the guise of "marriage," i.e., a marriage outside the bounds of scriptural authorization. Jesus taught that the person who divorces his/her spouse, unless the divorce is on the basis of fornication, and then marries another, is committing adultery (Mt. 19:9). Another passage seems to suggest that a divorced woman, simply by the act of being "put away," becomes an adulteress (Mt. 5:32). That, of course, cannot be the meaning of the passage. (a) The sense may be that the "put away" woman is exposed to the temptation of finding a new partner, hence, becoming an adulteress. (b) Or, the meaning could be that the mere fact that she has been divorced by her husband may lead many to suspect that she has committed adultery, hence, hang that reputation upon her. Adultery is a forgivable sin, provided the sinful activity is *discontinued*, and God's pardon is sought in the divinely prescribed fashion (1 Cor. 6:9-11).

ADVOCATE

The apostle John affirms that Jesus functions as an "advocate" on behalf of his people (1 Jn. 2:1). The Greek word for advocate is *parakletos*, literally suggesting the sense "to call to one's side." The term denotes "one who appears on behalf of another." While Satan is the adversary who is ever ready to accuse God's people (Rev. 12:10), Jesus, as our "attorney," is always on hand to plead the case of his disciples who strive to *walk continuously* in the light of divine instruction (1 Jn. 1:7).

AGNOSTIC

The word "agnostic" does not appear in the English Bible. The term derives, however, from Greek roots suggesting the idea "not known." When Paul visited the city of Athens, he noted that the pagans there had erected an altar to an "unknown" (*agnostos*) god (Acts 17:23). The apostle "took his text" from that inscription and proclaimed to them the *known* God! Paul used a kindred form of the word in his epistle to the saints at Corinth when he charged that some have "no knowledge" (*agnosia*) of God (1 Cor. 15:34). Peter employed the same term for the "ignorance" of certain foolish men (1 Pet. 2:15). In a philosophical sense, the term "agnostic" asserts the idea that there is insufficient evidence to confidently affirm the existence of God, hence, man cannot know, one way or the other, whether there is a supreme Being. Such an ideology was not endorsed by the great personalities of scripture (cf. Psa. 46:10; 2 Tim. 1:12), and it ignores a vast library of evidence that testifies otherwise.

AMOS, BOOK OF

Amos was a prophet in the northern kingdom of Israel in those days before the fall of Samaria (722/21 B.C.), the capital city. He cries out against the idolatry and wickedness of his people. He warns of a judgment that will come upon Israel and certain pagan peoples. He also provides a prophetic preview of the establishment of Christ's kingdom – the raising up of "the tabernacle of David" (9:11; cf. Acts 15:16).

ANGEL

The English "angel" is an anglicized form of the Greek *aggelos* (pronounced *angelos*). The term signifies a "messenger." *Aggelos* is used in several ways in the Scriptures. (a) It commonly denotes a heavenly order of created beings (Psa. 148:2, 5), who are "spirits" as to their nature, and who carry out the will of God on behalf of his people (Heb. 1:14). In Bible times, angels were visible on occasion (Acts 10:3; 12:7ff). Such manifestations are not evident today; miraculous events have ceased (1 Cor. 13:8-10). (b) The word may be used of a human messenger who serves as an envoy. John the Baptist, for example, was God's "messenger" (Mt. 11:10; Mk. 1:2). (c) The word may be employed *figuratively* of a providentially permitted physical malady (2 Cor. 12:7). (d) The "angels" of the churches of Asia may have been messengers who were in contact with John while the apostle was on the island of Patmos (Rev. 1:20).

ANGEL OF THE LORD

A careful consideration of the various texts in the Old Testament that mention the "angel of the LORD" (KJV), or the "angel of Jehovah" (ASV), reveal that this being was not of the *ordinary angel* class. He promised to multiply Hagar's seed, and she confessed, "You are a God who sees" (Gen. 16:10, 13). The "messenger" said to Abraham, "By myself I have sworn, *says Jehovah*" (Gen. 22:15-16). He identified himself as "the God of Bethel" (Gen. 31:11, 13). The "messenger" was both *distinct from* God, and yet he clearly possessed the *traits of deity*. A very strong case can be made for the view that this person was the preincarnate Word (Jn. 1:1), who became flesh in the form of Jesus Christ (Jn. 1:14). John the Baptizer was to prepare the way for the "messenger of the covenant" (Mal. 3:1), which, according to the New Testament, was Christ (Mt. 11:10). Jehovah promised Israel that his "angel" (messenger) would be with them in the wilderness (Ex. 23:20ff), and Paul speaks of the presence of Jesus on behalf of the nation as they wandered in Sinai (1 Cor. 10:4).

ANNIHILATION

The doctrine of "annihilation" is the idea that eventually, after a sufficient period of punishment, the souls of the wicked will go *out of existence*. This dogma is without biblical support. The punishment of those who die estranged from God is described as: "fire unquenchable" (Mt. 3:12). Final punishment is a state where "their worm dies not" and the "fire is not quenched" (Mk. 9:48). Upon the lost person, the wrath of God "abides" (present tense – *keeps on* abiding) (Jn. 3:36). Various figures are employed, in connection with the words "forever" or "everlasting," e.g., chains, contempt, destruction, torment (see Dan. 12:2; Mt. 18:8; 25:41, 46; 2 Thes. 1:9; Jude 6-7; Rev. 14:11; 19:3; 20:10). It is not the mere *effect* of punishment that is eternal, but the *actual* punishment itself (Mt. 25:46).

ANOINT

In the Old Testament, anointing with oil was used ceremonially to set apart special roles – especially that of prophets (1 Kgs. 19:16), priests (Ex. 28:41), and kings (1 Sam. 9:16). The most common Hebrew word for "anoint" is *mashah*, from which will come the term Messiah. The Greek word for "anoint" is *chrio*, the root from which "Christ" derives. Jesus becomes the "anointed One" (see Acts 10:38), because in him is happily combined the roles of prophet (Jn. 4:19; Acts 3:22ff), priest (Zech. 6:12-13; Heb. 3:1), and king (Mt. 2:2; Lk. 1:32-33; Acts 2:30ff). As prophet, Christ is the spokesman for God (Jn. 1:18); as priest, he offered his blood for atonement (Heb. 9:14); as king, he reigns at the right hand of God (1 Pet. 3:22).

ANTHROPOMORPHISM

This is the name of a figure of speech whereby God is described in human terms. The word derives from the Greek *anthropos* (man), and *morphe* (form), hence man-form. Because God is "spirit" (Jn. 4:24), and we are not capable of understanding spirit qualities, the Scriptures accommodate our level of comprehension by the use of symbolism. Hence, biblical writers speak of the hands, eyes, etc. of God (Isa. 59:1-2; Heb. 4:13). It is an erroneous notion to contend, as Mormons do, that God is literally a physical being (cf. Hos. 11:9; Mt. 16:17).

ANTICHRIST

The Greek term *antikristos* is found five times in the New Testament – all references being in John's writings (1 Jn. 2: 18, 22; 4:3; 2 Jn. 7). The meaning literally is "against Christ." John warns that there were "many" (1 Jn. 2:18; 2 Jn. 2:7) of these false teachers in his day (see "even now" – 1 Jn. 2: 18; 4:3). The term cannot be, therefore, an allusion to some mysterious, Satanic leader who is to appear shortly before the return of Christ, as that theory is advocated by those of the dispensational/premillennial persuasion. The expression is generic, denoting any dogma that is *against* Christ – in terms of truth *regarding* him (e.g., a denial of his deity), or opposition to truth which has issued *from* him. See also: DISPENSATIONALISM.

ANTITYPE

Though this word is not found in most English translations of the New Testament, the thought is there in the Greek text. It is an anglicized form of the original term *antitupos*. The term is rendered "like-figure" (1 Pet. 3:21) and "figure" (Heb. 9: 24). Literally, a *tupos* was a mark, or impression, produced by a blow (cf. Jn. 20:25). The antitype, therefore, is that which stands over against, or corresponds to, the type. The Old Testament contains many "types" or "shadows" which find their reality (fulfillment) in Christ. The Passover lamb was a type of Christ (Jn. 1:29; 1 Cor. 5:7). Moses was a type of Christ (Dt. 18:

15ff; Acts 3:22). In 1 Peter 3:21, the apostle argues that Noah's salvation from a wicked world, by means of water, pictured our deliverance from the guilt of sin, by means of immersion in water (i.e., when one, with penitent faith, submits to baptism). Noah's salvation was the *type*; ours is the *antitype*. See: TYPE.

APOCALYPTIC

Apocalyptic language is a form of expression that is highly symbolic. Ideas are conveyed by vivid figures of speech. When the figures are interpreted, the meaning of the message is *uncovered*. The word derives from the Greek *apokalupto*, meaning to uncover, to unveil. The first word of the final book of the New Testament is *apokalupsis*, "revelation," which serves as the title of the book. Thus, this book sometimes is called the Apocalypse. Certain portions of Daniel, Ezekiel, and Zechariah are apocalyptic in nature, as are sections of Matthew 24. And then, of course, the book of Revelation is significantly of this nature. This type of symbolism was employed in times of danger. The message, by means of word-pictures, could be "smuggled" to the people of God, thus affording them great comfort. At the same time, the celebration of ultimate victory over their enemies would be concealed from the hostile opposition.

APOCRYPHA

This word originally meant "hidden things," and it suggested a special body of information reserved for a select group. Eventually, it came to signify a collection of fourteen or fifteen books, some of which are included in some editions of the

English Bible – especially the versions distributed under the auspices of the Roman Catholic Church. The Roman Church subscribes to the idea that several of the apocryphal books are inspired of God and thus should be embraced within the sacred Canon. These are: Tobit, Judith, Wisdom of Solomon, Ecclesiasticus, Baruch, I and II Macabees, together with fragments of Daniel and Esther. The evidence is against acknowledging these books as *inspired.* (a) These works were not in the Hebrew Old Testament. (b) They were produced *between* those eras in which inspired Testaments were being given, i.e., in the inter-testament period (see Josephus, *Against Apion* 1.8). (c) Neither Jesus nor the apostles regarded these documents as inspired of God. (d) The books make no claim of inspiration. (e) They contain numerous inaccuracies and contradictions. (f) The moral tone of the books is far below that of the Bible. While they provide some interesting historical data of the inter-biblical period, they are not products of divine inspiration.

APOLOGETICS

This word is an anglicized form of the Greek, *apologeia*, literally meaning, "a verbal defense." It is found eight times in the N.T. (a verb form occurs some ten times). For example, Luke uses this word to describe Paul's defense of the Christian system before various rulers (Acts 22:1; 24:10; 25:8; 26:1). In the modern world, the term takes on the sense of making a reasoned defense of such matters as: the existence of God, the divine origin of mankind, the inspiration of the Scriptures, the deity of Christ. Apologetics constitutes one of the most vital areas of biblical study, for without a solid faith-foundation, all else fails.

APOSTASY

Apostasy is an English term that reflects the Greek *apotasia*. Originally it meant to desert one's post; it was used of political revolt. In the Old Testament the word is employed of turning away from following the way of God (see Josh. 22:22 – LXX; see LXX entry). In the New Testament *apostasia* describes a massive "falling away" from the truth of the gospel resulting in the revealing of the "man of sin," who is also the "son of perdition" (2 Thes. 2:1ff). This opposing force, which was already beginning in Paul's day, and which exalts itself mightily against God, will be destroyed by Christ at the time of his return. The idea that a child of God, or a conglomerate of Christians, can never so sin as to be lost, though popular in the community of "Christendom," is without biblical substance, and is terribly dangerous (see Gal. 5:4; 1 Tim. 4:1ff; 2 Tim. 4: 1ff; Heb. 3:12; 2 Pet. 2:1).

APOSTLE

This word is related to a Greek verb, *apostello*, meaning "to send away, to send forth." It is used in several senses in the New Testament. (a) Christ was God's "apostle," sent from heaven to reveal the divine will and to provide atonement for sin (Heb. 3:1). (b) The term is used of a select group of men chosen by Jesus to do a special work on his behalf. First there was the Twelve. Of these Judas perished (Jn. 17:12; Acts 1:25) and was replaced by Matthias (Acts 1:21ff). Finally Paul was selected as an apostle, "out of due season" (Acts 9:15;1 Cor. 15: 8). (c) The word was also used of others in a *generic* sense, i.e., of messengers who were assigned various duties. Among these were Barnabas (Acts 14:4, 14), and Silvanus and Timothy (1 Thes. 2:6). There are no "apostles" today, in the special sense

A Practical Handbook

of the Twelve and Paul, and claims of such (e.g., in Mormonism) are fallacious.

ARMAGEDDON

The name "Armageddon" is derived from a passage in the book of Revelation, where certain opposing forces were gathered at a place called Har-Magedon for a great battle (Rev. 16:16). It is believed that the original term pertained to "the hill of Megiddo," a place in northwestern Palestine. It was the most famous battlefield of ancient history, very prominent in Old Testament literature (see Jdgs. 4:13ff; Jdgs. 7; 2 Kgs. 23:29). It was at this place that Deborah and the small army of Israel overcame the powerful military forces of Sisera. This incident probably serves as the backdrop for the symbolic use of the term in Revelation. It seems to serve as a prophetic clue for the great victory that Christ and his armies will enjoy on the final day of earth's history when the forces of evil are vanquished forever (see Rev. 19:11ff). The imagery of Revelation 16:12ff, "frogs," etc., clearly reflects the *symbolic* nature of the description. There is no basis in this context for an actual military conflict that is supposed to occur (according to dispensational theology) just before an alleged 1,000 year reign of Christ upon the earth. See: DISPENSATIONALISM.

ASTROLOGY

Astrology is a pagan superstition that holds that heavenly bodies influence human activity, together with the theory that human events can be predicted by "reading" the stars. This mythology is condemned in the Scriptures (Dt. 18:10-12; 2 Kgs. 23:5; Isa. 47:13-14; Jer. 10:2; Gal. 5:19-20). Astrology is antagonistic to the Christian system; it encourages a fatalistic viewpoint of life and discourages the development of the noblest qualities of which man is capable. Furthermore, it has no basis in science. A secular encyclopedia states: "Astrology, in spite of attempts to establish itself as a science, must be considered a pseudo-science and a divinatory art."

ATHEISM

From *a* (meaning "no") and *theos* ("God"). It is a word that depicts the irrational ideology of the person who dogmatically says: "There is no God" (cf. Psa. 14:1). To be an atheist one must believe that the Universe is either eternal or self-caused – neither of which views is supported by the evidence. Science testifies that the Universe had a beginning (Second Law of Thermodynamics), and there is no evidence to suggest that a material object has the ability to create itself (First Law of Thermodynamics). Atheism asserts that this marvelous planet upon which we live, which is so intricately designed, is but an accident resulting from the forces of nature (yet see Rom. 1:20). If logically pursued, atheism argues that there is no such thing as morality; rather, every person is his own "god," to craft the rules of right and wrong. After all, it is claimed, man is but the product of the blind forces of nature (evolutionary processes). Atheist Jean Paul Sartre argued that since there is no God, nothing is wrong. Every choice that man makes is right. This senseless philosophy has brought much misery to humankind.

ATONEMENT

The English word "atonement" derives from an Anglo-Saxon term which, practically speaking, signifies "a making at one." Though the English term "atonement" is common to the Old Testament, the word is found only once in the New Testament (Rom. 5:11 KJV). There the original term (*katallage*), is better rendered "reconciliation" (ASV; cf. also 2 Cor. 5:19). The Greek word denotes the "reestablishment of an interrupted or broken relationship." In the biblical context, atonement has to do with the plan employed by the Lord to provide a way of salvation for sinful humanity by means of the redemptive mission of Christ. Here are the basic facts. (a) God is a perfectly holy being (Isa. 6:3; Rev. 4:8); sin, therefore, is contrary to his very nature (Jas. 1:13). As a truly holy Being, the Lord cannot ignore sin, or tolerate wickedness indefinitely, in any form (Hab. 1:13). (b) Jehovah is also a God of justice – the very foundation of his rule (Psa. 89:14). Accordingly, some satisfaction for sin must be made. The principle is this: "The wages of sin is death" (Rom. 6:23). (c) If, therefore, man was to be redeemed, God would have to extend mercy (cf. Eph. 2:4) in some fashion whereby divine justice could be satisfied. Exactly how was that to be achieved? (d) The solution is realized in the gift of Christ. Jesus lived the perfect life (Jn. 8:29; Heb. 4:15; 1 Pet. 2:22), and therefore became *qualified* to function as a substitute offering on man's behalf (cf. Heb. 2:10; 5:8-9). Through Jesus' death, Heaven's requirement of justice is satisfied (see Isa. 53:11; Rom. 3:22ff). Hence, the atoning offering of the Son of God became available to all men (Isa. 53:6; Jn. 3:16; 1 Tim. 2:4; 2 Pet. 3:9). (Note: The Calvinistic dogma of a "limited" atonement – only for an "elect" group chosen before the foundation of the world – is quite erroneous. (e) Jesus is the author of eternal salvation to all who obey him (Jn. 3:36; Rom. 6:17-18; Heb.

5:8-9). One is reconciled to God when he, through obedience, accepts Christ as his "atonement" offering.

AUTHORITY

The most popular Greek word for "authority" is *exousia* (sometimes translated as "power"). The term, with a variety of usages, is found 102 times in the New Testament. The word, together with some parallel terms, are employed of: (a) The authority of God (Lk. 12:5; Rom. 9:21; Jude 25). God's authority is his sovereign right to do anything consistent with his nature and will. (b) Divine authority was exercised by Christ (Mk. 2:10; Mt. 28:18). (c) Jesus bestowed a certain authority to his apostles (Lk. 10:19; cf. Mt. 19:28). (d) A measure of authority is granted to the civil rulers to maintain order in society (Rom. 13:1-7). (e) There is an order of authority resulting from the creation of man and woman. Man is the "head" of woman (1 Cor. 11:3), who must acknowledge his "authority" in church worship (1 Cor. 11:10; cf. 1 Tim. 2:12). (f) There is a chain of authority in the home; the husband is the "head" of the wife (Eph. 5:22ff), and children are to obey their parents (Eph. 6:1). (g) In churches where men are qualified (1 Tim. 3:1ff; Tit. 1:5ff), elders (pastors, shepherds, bishops) exercise a certain persuasive level of authority (1 Thes. 5:12; Heb. 13:17). The notion that there is a successor to the apostles (a pope), who exercises authority over the church on earth, is contradicted by Scripture (Mt. 28:18; Eph. 1:22-23). (h) The Holy Scriptures, being inspired of God and buttressed with abundant evidence as to their divine origin, likewise carry an authoritative force (1 Cor. 4:6; 2 Tim. 3:16-17; 2 Tim. 4:1ff).

AUTONOMY

This word derives of two roots, *auto* ("self"), and *nomos* ("law"). The term can have either a negative or positive connotation. (a) Man is not autonomous, i.e., he is not empowered to rule himself (cf. Jer. 10:23). He is a creature of God, and the Lord has a "right" over him (Rom. 9:21). See: SOVEREIGNTY. (b) Each local congregation of the church of Christ is independent, thus, autonomous. There is no pope, cardinal, or conference that exercises autocratic authority over a local church with divine approval. While "bishops" (see this reference) have authority in the area of EXPEDIENCY (see), only Christ has full authority over his church in issues of teaching and practice. In modern cases where churches are incorporated for legal protection, the "board members" or "trustees" function only as legal representatives on behalf of the church membership; they do not exercise any sort of autonomous authority.

BACKSLIDING

This is an expression used frequently in the Old Testament to describe those who forsook their loyalty to God and began to serve Satan again. No fewer than thirteen times the prophet Jeremiah rebuked ancient Israel for her backsliding ways (Jer. 2:19; 3:6; cf. Hos. 4:16 KJV; 11:7). It is useless to argue, as Calvinists do, that backsliding is inconsequential in terms of one's eternal salvation. Apostasy results in "destruction" (2 Pet. 2:2).

BAPTISM

The noun "baptism" and the corresponding verb, "baptize," come directly from Greek to English with only slight spelling modification. The word, used literally, denotes *to immerse, dip*, or *submerge*. When employed metaphorically, it suggests the idea of being *overwhelmed*. There are several senses it can take in the New Testament, depending upon the context. (a) It was used with reference to the overwhelming suffering that Christ would endure at Calvary (Lk. 12:50). (b) "Baptism" describes the extraordinary measure of the outpouring of the Holy Spirit, received by the apostles on Pentecost (Acts 1:5; 2:4), and later by the first Gentiles to whom the gospel was extended (Acts 11: 15-17). (c) It is symbolically used to describe the punishment of hell (Mt. 3:10-12). (d) The most common use of baptism has to do with an immersion in water as an act of spiritual obedience. It was introduced first by John the Baptizer (Mt. 3:6), and subsequently administered by Jesus' disciples (Jn. 4:1-2). Finally it was authorized under the "great commission" (Mt. 28:19-20; Mk. 16:15-16). The baptism of the Christian age embodies: immersion in water (Acts 8:38-39; Rom. 6:3-4; Col. 2:12), for a person who has the ability and willingness to both believe the gospel message and repent of sin (Mk. 16:16; Acts 2:38). The purpose of the ordinance is for the acquisition of pardon (Acts 2:38; 22:16; 1 Pet. 3:21). At baptism one enters a relationship with Jesus Christ (Rom. 6:3-4; Gal. 3:26-27) and becomes a part of the Lord's spiritual body (1 Cor. 12:13), the church (Eph. 1:22-23; Col. 1:18, 24). This is the same realm known as the kingdom of God, which is entered by the "new birth" process (Jn. 3:3-5). The modern practices of "baptizing" infants, "sprinkling" water as a substitute for immersion, and baptizing people who labor under the illusion that God, for Christ's sake, has *already* forgiven them – finds no support in the New Testament. Water immersion is the "one baptism" (Eph. 4:5) that continues to the end of time (cf. Mt. 28:19-20).

BAPTISM FOR THE DEAD

The practice of baptism "for the dead" is mentioned once in the New Testament. "If the dead are not raised at all, why then are they baptized for them?" (1 Cor. 15:29). Though the passage is somewhat obscure, several things are evident: (a) It gives no sanction to the modern practice (by Mormons) of proxy baptism, i.e., a living person being baptized so that some dead person can receive salvation. That idea would contradict numerous passages. For example, the consequences of neither obedience nor disobedience are *transferable* to others (see Ezek. 18:20). Each person must give account of *his own* conduct (Rom. 14:12; 2 Cor. 5:10). Those who die unprepared will meet the Lord in that fashion (Mt. 25:1ff; Heb. 9:27). Moreover, it is impossible, after death, to alter one's destiny (see Lk. 16:26). (b) This controversial passage is obviously an *ad hominem* argument (one designed to expose the inconsistency of an opponent) intended to counter the claim of some at Corinth that "there is no resurrection of the dead" (1 Cor. 15:12). In some way it shows that if there is to be no resurrection from the dead, it is useless to continue practicing baptism. The sense may be: "If the dead will never be raised, why do these false teachers continue practicing baptism – the very form of which pictures a resurrection from a grave?"

BEGINNING

A word that denotes the commencement of every thing that has a point of origin. The "heavens and the earth" had a beginning (Gen. 1:1), hence, are not eternal. Material origins must be explained *supernaturally* since there is no known naturalistic explanation. When the Universe experienced its "beginning," the eternal Word (Jn. 1:1), identified as the preincarnate Christ (Jn. 1:14), was already existing (cf. Jn. 8:58). Christ, therefore, was not a "created" being, as "Jehovah's Witnesses" contend. The human family has existed since "the beginning of the creation" (Mk. 10:6), i.e., our origin occurred in the same week (Gen. 1; Ex. 20:11). This contradicts the evolutionary theory that humankind arrived upon the earth billions of years after the initial creation.

BEGOTTEN

Literally, this term has to do with the implantation of "seed" by which a child is conceived. The word is *figuratively* used in Scripture to illustrate the spiritual agency, namely the *word of God*, by which one becomes a believer in Christ. When Paul preached the gospel to the people of Corinth (Acts 18:5ff; cf. 1 Cor. 15:1-4), leading to their conversion (Acts 18:8), he is said to have "begotten" these folks (1 Cor. 4:15; see 1 Pet. 1:23). When faith acts in obedience to other commands, e.g., repentance and baptism (Acts 2:38), the person has been "born" anew (Jn. 3:3-5) and may be characterized as one "begotten [or "born"] of God" (1 Jn. 5:1 ASV/KJV).

BELIEF

"Belief" is the noun form of the verb "believe." True belief embraces several important elements. (a) Belief embodies an intellectual awareness of certain theological and historical realities. Though God is neither visibly nor audibly manifested to us, belief in him is not grounded in superstition, or a blind "leap into the dark." Rather, it is based upon a critical use of the mind in the evaluation of evidence (Psa. 19:1ff; Rom. 1:20). Faith in Christ is anchored in the reliability of the historical evidence concerning his life and teaching. (b) Belief also involves a willingness to trust God and place confidence in his Son. (Note: Sometimes the Greek word for "belief" is translated "trust" – see John 2:24 ASV.) The word can carry the idea of "committing one's self to another on the basis of trust" (cf. Lk. 16:11; 1 Tim. 1:11). (c) While many think that the foregoing elements exhaust the meaning of "belief," that does not represent the truth. True belief expresses itself in *doing* the will of God. Sometimes believing is paralleled with obeying (cf. Jn. 3:36 ASV; cf. Heb. 3:18-19). A careful consideration of "belief" in the book of Acts reveals that the term includes the idea of obeying the requirements of the gospel plan. Compare Acts 2:38, 41, with 44. Note how "believed" and "disobedient" stand in contrast in Acts 14:1-2. Consider how the verb "believed" embraced "baptized" in Acts 19:2-3. Faith, therefore, that refuses to manifest itself in obedience is an unavailing, dead faith (Jas. 2:14ff).

BIBLE

An English word which means "scroll" or "book." It is used of the sixty-six documents that comprise the book of Scripture – thirty-nine O.T. narratives; twenty-seven N.T. books (sometimes called the two covenants – Ex. 24:7; Mt. 26:28; Heb. 8:7). The O.T. (written in Hebrew and Aramaic) contains books of *law* (Genesis through Deuteronomy), *history* (Joshua through Esther), *poetry* (Job through Song of Solomon) and *prophecy* (Isaiah through Malachi). The N.T. (written in Greek) has four books of *biography* (Matthew through John), an *historical* narrative (Acts), twenty-one *epistles*, or letters (Romans through Jude), and one book of *prophecy* (Revelation). There is a vast amount of evidence, e.g., the unity of the documents, the miraculous prophetic utterances, the precise historical accuracy, etc., which establishes beyond reasonable doubt the Bible's claim that it is the revelation of God to humankind (see 2 Tim. 3:16-17). This book provides man with a record of his origin (Gen. 2:7), his general mission (Eccl. 12:13-14), and his ultimate destiny (Mt. 25:46), depending upon his obedience or disobedience.

BISHOP

This is one of the titles of a church official who, in the company of fellow bishops (always a plurality of men), oversees a local congregation of Christ's church. "Bishop" translates the Greek term *episcopos*, literally "oversee." The bishop is the same as an elder (*presbuteros* – older man) (see Acts 20:17; 28), which means he is also identified as a "shepherd" or "pastor" (*poimen* - one who tends, feeds, and protects) (cf. Eph. 4:11). Peter uses forms of all three of these terms in 1 Peter 5:1-2, when he instructs the *elders* to *tend* the flock among them, within which they exercise the *oversight* (cf. Heb. 13:17). The qualifications of these officers are found mainly in 1 Timothy 3 and Titus 1. The notion that a "bishop" is over a large area of the church (as in the dogma of Catholicism) is foreign to the Scriptures.

BLASPHEMY

This word comes directly from the Greek, *blasphemeo*, which is believed to derive from *blapto* (to injure) and *pheme* (speech), hence, injurious speech. Scripture speaks of those who blaspheme God (Rom. 2:24; 1 Tim. 6:1). It is also possible to blaspheme Christ, as certain hateful ones did at the cross when they "reviled" or "railed on" (*blasphemeo*) the Lord (Mt. 27:39; Lk. 22:65). One must be cautious that he does not conduct himself in such a way as to cause the "word of God" to be blasphemed (Tit. 2:5; cf. 1 Tim. 6:1). Either by teaching falsely, or by a corrupt style of living, one who professes loyalty to God may cause sacred things to be spoken against. The controversial passage about "blasphemy against the Spirit" (Mt. 12:31) has troubled many because, in some sense, it suggests that this transgression is beyond forgiveness. However, inasmuch as pardon for *all* sin is elsewhere promised (1 Jn. 1:9), this warning must refer to those who utterly reject the Spirit's message (as now made known through the Scriptures – Eph. 6:17), hence, and place themselves beyond the only redemptive means available for their salvation. Paul, in his early life, was a blasphemer (1 Tim. 1:13), but his sins were washed away when he submitted to Heaven's saving plan (Acts 22:16).

BLOOD

Blood is a prominent theme in the Bible. Because blood is the life-stream of a person (Lev. 17:11), it becomes the biblical representation for "life." Since man, by virtue of sin has forfeited the right to live (Gen. 2:17; Rom. 6:23; Eph. 2:1), in order to satisfy the justice of God, a blood-offering was required (Heb. 9:22). The blood of animals, however, could not accomplish the ultimate objective, though it was used in the preparatory phase of Jehovah's redemptive plan (Heb. 10:4). Jesus, as the lamb of God (Jn. 1:29), took upon himself human nature (flesh and blood), that he might be able to die for sin (Heb. 2:9, 14; 9:14; 10:19). Accordingly, through the shedding of his blood, redemption is obtainable for those who are "in" him (Eph. 1:7). This blessing is achieved when the penitent believer is immersed into Christ (Rom. 6:3-4; Gal. 3:26-27; cf. Heb. 9:14; Eph. 5:26; 1 Pet. 3:21). When the Christian observes the weekly, Lord's-day communion, he focuses in part upon the shedding of Jesus' blood (Mt. 26:26-29).

BODY

The term "body" is used in Scripture in both a literal sense and in a figurative sense. (a) In a *literal* sense, it is employed of the physical "tabernacle" in which the spirit of man dwells (2 Cor. 5:1ff). The human body was fashioned on the sixth day of the creation week from the dust of the ground (Gen. 2:7; Eccl. 12:7; 1 Cor. 15:47), and it returns to the dust when the spirit departs (Jas. 2:26). It is a magnificently designed structure that bears witness to its creator (Psa. 139:14; 1 Cor. 12:18); to suggest that it developed from the blind forces of nature by evolutionary processes defies all logic. The future resurrection of the body, in a different *spiritual* form, is a fundamental Bible truth (Dan. 12:2; Jn. 5:28-29; Acts 24:15; Phil. 3:21; Heb. 6:2). (b) "Body" is used *symbolically* for the "church." At the point of baptism, one enters the "body" (1 Cor. 12:13). That "body" consists of many "members," yet it is "one" in its essential composition (1 Cor. 12:12; Eph. 4:4). The expression "one body" is the equivalent of "one church" (Eph. 1:22-23; Col. 1:18, 24). While there may be many congregations that make up that one body (Rev. 1:4), the modern idea of many denominations is a manifestation of apostasy from gospel truth. The imagery of the "body" further suggests that all direction to the "members" is received from the "head," Christ (Eph. 5:23; Col. 1:18). Moreover, if the body is to function as God intended, unity among its members must prevail (cf. 1 Cor. 12:12ff).

BORN IN SIN

The most commonly misapplied passage, in support of the idea that children are "born in sin," is Psalm 51:5. For a number of reasons, this text cannot be teaching that infants are *actually* born sinful; such a view would contradict numerous other passages of Scripture. See: INFANTS. What, then, does this passage from Psalms teach? There are several possible views. (a) Since Psalm 51 is one of David's penitent psalms, revealing the anguish resulting from his adulterous conduct with Bathsheba, some have felt that verse 5 contains words that are *figuratively* put into the mouth of the child conceived by that illicit union (2 Sam. 11:5). This imagery would highlight the sinfulness of that relationship. In that case, the sin would be attributed to the parent, not the child. (b) Others have suggested that David alludes to an incident in his ancestral lineage, an adulterous affair (Gen. 38), whereby he was considered *ceremonially* defiled because he was of the 10th generation of that unlawful intercourse (Dt. 23:2). This is probably only a remote possibility. (c) Most likely Psalms 51:5 refers merely to the fact that David *was born into a sinful environment.* We are all conceived in, and brought forth into, a sinful world. But we do not *actually* sin until we arrive at a state of spiritual *responsibility.* Perhaps David also, by the use of dramatic language, alludes to the fact that sin had characterized his whole life, *relatively speaking.* In a similarly poetic section, for example, Job, in denying that he had neglected his benevolent responsibilities, affirmed that he had cared for the orphan and the widow *from his mother's womb* (Job 31:18). Surely, no one believes that from the day of his birth Job was out ministering to the needy! In fact, the Hebrew parallelism of this verse clearly indicates that the word "womb" is used in the sense of "youth." (d) Those who employ Psalm 51:5 to buttress the doctrine that sin is inherited from one's mother are faced with a serious problem. Jesus was both conceived by, and brought forth from, a human mother (Lk. 1:31). If original sin is inherited from one's mother, Christ was "tainted." If, however, someone should suggest that depravity is received only from the father, then Psalm 51:5 cannot be used to prove it, for it mentions only the *mother!*

BREAKING BREAD

On the night before his death, during the Passover celebration, Jesus instituted the "communion" supper for his disciples (Mt. 26:26ff; Mk. 14:22ff; Lk. 22:19ff; cf. 1 Cor. 11:23ff). The "Lord's supper" consisted of two elements – bread and fruit of the vine. Later, however, the expression "breaking bread" is used as a figure of speech (known as synecdoche – the part for the whole) that represents the entire communion celebration – involving both components (cf. Acts 2:42; 20:7; cf. 1 Cor. 10:16-17). The "breaking of bread" that was associated with the "communion," though, must be distinguished from a common meal taken for physical nourishment, to which reference is made in some contexts (Lk. 24:30; Acts 2:46; 20:11).

BROTHER, BRETHREN

The term "brother" is from the Greek *adelphos*, which technically signifies "from the same womb." The word is used in different senses in the New Testament. (a) It is employed literally of siblings of the same *parents* (Acts 12:2). (b) It can denote those of the same *nation* (Acts 2:29; 9:17; 22:5). Ananias' use of "brother" with reference to Saul does not imply that the persecutor was already a Christian prior to having his sins "washed away" (Acts 22:16). (c) The most common form in the N.T. has to do with those who have shared in a common *new birth* process (Jn. 3:3-5), and who are, therefore, *kinsman in the Lord* (see Phil. 1:14; 4:1; Col. 1:2; 1 Thes. 5:27; Philem. 16). It is not appropriate to refer to those as "brethren," who nominally profess an identification with Christianity, but who have not genuinely obeyed the gospel of Christ (2 Thes. 1:8; 1 Pet. 4:17).

CALL, CALLING

The Christian commitment is biblically designated as a "calling." The divine "calling" (Eph. 4:1) is not a *direct communication* from God or his Holy Spirit, as some today allege. No one on earth knows *anything* about Jesus Christ, and his way of redemption, except what they have learned either directly, or indirectly, from the Scriptures. Here are some facts about the Christian's calling: (a) Its source is God (Acts 2:39; Heb. 3:1). (b) It is characterized by a humble, willing-to-learn attitude (1 Cor. 1:26-29). (c) The sacred calling is by means of the gospel (2 Thes. 2:14). (d) Its design is for a holy, worthy life (1 Cor. 1:2; Eph. 4:1). (e) Its direction is upward (Phil. 3:14). (f) Its sphere of operation is "in Christ" (Phil. 3:14). (g) The ultimate hope of the calling is in a single destiny – heaven (Eph. 4:4;

Col. 1:5). It is not without significance that the Greek word that is normally rendered "church," in our English versions, is *ekklesia*, a compound term meaning "to call" and "out from." Such emphasizes the Christian's separation from his past life of worldliness.

CATHOLIC

This term originates with a Greek word, *katholikos*, which means "general" or "universal." The expression is not found in the Scriptures, but it has been employed in various senses in church history. (a) Justin Martyr (*Dialog* lxxxi) used the term for the "general" resurrection of the dead at the end of time. (b) In later history, the Western church (Rome) adopted this descriptive to distinguish itself from the East (the Greek Orthodox movement). Today, the Roman Catholic Church applies the title exclusively to itself. In his debate with Bishop John Purcell, Alexander Campbell argued that the "Holy Roman Catholic Church" is neither holy, Roman, catholic, or, in a legitimate sense, the church. (c) Catholic is sometimes applied to seven of the N.T. epistles that were more "general" in the recipients addressed, than some of the other letters. These are: James, 1 Peter, 2 Peter, 1, 2, 3 John, and Jude.

CELIBACY

This word derives from a Latin term meaning "unmarried." The *ideal*, in the divine scheme of things, is for human beings to marry (Gen. 2:18; 1 Tim. 5:14). On occasion, it is not advisable to marry, such as in times of severe persecution (1 Cor. 7: 26, 35, 40). Even then, however, marriage is not a sin (1 Cor. 7:36). Nor is remaining single sinful. An *eligible* person may marry at any time, and to *forbid* a legitimate marital union is a mark of apostasy (1 Tim. 4:1ff). The dogma that the celibate state is holier than the married state is based in religious superstition, not Scripture.

CHRIST

The title "Christ" was applied to Jesus of Nazareth because he was the fulfillment of the Old Testament prophecies pertaining to the coming "Messiah." Jesus was previewed as the Messiah by the prophets (Psa. 2:1ff; Dan. 9:25-27). He personally affirmed that he was the promised Christ (Jn. 4:25-26; Mk. 14:61-62). Because of his miracles and teaching, the disciples became convinced he was the Christ (Mt. 16:16). Even many of those involved in his crucifixion came to believe that he is the Messiah (see Acts 2:29ff). There is no legitimate reason today for any Jewish person to reject Jesus of Nazareth as the promised Messiah of O.T. literature; only bias obscures their vision of the evidence (2 Cor. 3:14ff). See also: ANOINT.

CHRISTIAN

This is the name given to the disciples of Christ in Antioch of Syria following the first missionary journey of Paul and Barnabas (Acts 11:26). The verb *chrematizo* ("called") in this passage suggests a *divinely given* appellation. Some think that "called" also is a technical term that hints that it was a disciple's "business" to serve Christ (W.E. Vine). Herod Agrippa II, a ruler before whom Paul appeared, declared that the apostle, with forceful persuasion, was making a case for becoming a Christian (Acts 26:28). And Peter proudly contended that those who suffer for the name "Christian" should glorify God thereby (1 Pet. 4:16). There is no reason to believe that the early Christians adopted the name for themselves, or that the appellation was thrust upon them by their enemies. It is a tragedy that this sacred title has been replaced today by so many sectarian designations (e.g., Catholic, Lutheran, Baptist, etc.).

CHRONICLES 1, BOOK OF

The purpose of this book is to re-acquaint the post-Babylonian captivity generation of Jews with the history of David's administration, thus, a period of about forty years. It places great interest upon the temple and priesthood during David's dynasty.

CHRONICLES 2, BOOK OF

This book surveys a period of some 424 years, from the beginning of Solomon's reign to the edict from the Persian king, Cyrus, who commissioned the Jews to return from the Babylonian captivity to re-establish their dominion in Canaan. He even furnished finance for the project. The book underscores the apostasy of the Lord's people during that historical era. In the Hebrew Bible, 1 and 2 Chronicles comprise one document.

CHRONOLOGY

Biblical chronology has to do with the relationship of the events recorded in Scripture to certain dates. Some events are a bit ambiguous in terms of date; others are more precise. While the Bible does not provide a precise date for the creation of the world, two things are clear: (a) Human history extends back to the very week of the creation of the Universe (Gen. 1;

Ex. 20:11; Mk. 10:6; Rom. 1:20). (b) The genealogical data in the biblical record limits man's longevity to a span of *thousands* of years, not millions – as per the evolutionary theory (Gen. 5; Lk. 3:23ff). (c) Other general dates are helpful. Abraham lived about 2000 years before Christ, and David reigned approximately 1,000 before Christ was born. Jesus was born around 5/4 B.C. (this reckoning takes into account an error in the early calendar), and it is now generally believed that he died in A.D. 30. The church was established on Pentecost, fifty days later. Paul was executed in Rome around A.D. 67. The city of Jerusalem was destroyed by the Romans in A.D. 70, and John penned the final book of the New Testament (Revelation) around A.D. 96.

CHURCH

The English word "church" is derived from the Greek *kurikon*, meaning "belonging to the Lord." The actual word in the Greek text, that stands behind the modern rendition, "church," is *ekklesia*, "called out." It is now generally conceded that the basic meaning of the term is "assembly" or "congregation." In a non-religious sense, the word was used of a public assembly (Acts 19:32, 39-40). In a *religious* sense, *ekklesia* was employed in the following ways: (a) It is used of the people of God *universally*, equivalent to the "one body" (Mt. 16:18; Eph. 4:4; Col. 1:18). (b) *Ekklesia* could signify the Lord's people in a *certain region* (Acts 9:31). (c) The term can embody a congregation of saints in a particular *city* (1 Cor. 1:2; Rev. 1:4). (d) It may refer to *gathering* of Christians in an assembled meeting (1 Cor. 14:34; 3 Jn. 10). This organism was in the mind of God from eternity (Eph. 3:10). It was foretold in the Old Testament (2 Sam. 7:12-13; Isa. 2:2-4; Dan. 2:44). It was promised by

Christ (Mt. 16:18), and established on Pentecost (Acts 2). The universal congregation will be received by Christ at the time of his second coming (Eph. 5:27; Rev. 21:2). There is no sanction in the Scriptures for the modern scheme of varying denominational churches. This very system militates against the work of Christ (see Jn. 17:20-21).

CITIZENSHIP

Citizenship is the legal relationship that one sustains to a city, state, or country. Paul was a citizen of Tarsus in Cilicia (Acts 21:39), and he enjoyed the privileges of "citizenship" in the Roman empire (Acts 22:28). His citizenship granted certain protective procedures (cf. 22:25), and the privilege of judicial review (Acts 25:11). The Christian has the right to use the resources of civil government for his protection (Rom. 13:1ff). "Citizenship" is used metaphorically in Philippians 3:20 to describe the heavenly status of those within the kingdom of Christ, the church.

COLOSSIANS, BOOK OF

Colossae was a city about 100 miles east of Ephesus. To the church in this city, Paul wrote a letter; it was one of his four "prison" epistles from Rome (Acts 28). The letter is both "doctrinal" and "practical." It deals principally with a heresy that threatened the saints in this city. The false doctrine had elements of both Judaism and Gnosticism (an erroneous concept alleging special knowledge from God). It involved such heretical ideas as the worship of angels (2:18). The apostle addresses this error, urges the brethren to exalt Christ, and to be faithful in their Christian living.

COMMISSION, GREAT

An expression commonly used of a special directive given by Christ in a post-resurrection appearance before he ascended back into heaven. The "commission" is found in three complimentary forms (Mt. 28:18-20; Mk. 16:15-16; Lk. 24:47-27). A harmony of its elements reveals the following factors: (a) There is the obligation for the followers of Christ to go forth preaching the basic components of the gospel, namely the facts about the identity of Jesus and his mission. (b) Their field of operation is to be world-wide, and the scope of the message is universal, i.e., to all men. (c) Obligations imposed upon those who hear the message are to believe it, repent of sin, and be immersed in water. (d) The resulting blessings are salvation from sin, and possession by, and intimate fellowship with, the Godhead – Father, Son, and Holy Spirit. While not historically parallel, John 3:3-5 (the new birth instruction) is highly complimentary to the "commission" passages.

COMMUNION

"Communion" is a term applied to the Lord's Supper because of its usage in 1 Corinthians 10:16. It emphasizes the fellowship (*koinonia* – sharing, participation) we enjoy with Christ when we partake of the sacred elements (cf. "with you" in Mt. 26:29). (a) The communion involves two elements – "bread" and "fruit of the vine" (Mt. 26:26-29 – not "water," as per Mormon doctrine); (b) It is a celebration "in remembrance" of the body and blood of the Savior (Lk. 22:19; 1 Cor. 11:25). The notion that the *actual* flesh and blood of Christ is present in the elements (*transubstantiation* – Catholic dogma; *consubstantiation* – Lutheran doctrine) is a mere human tradition of post-apostolic development. (c) The communion is authorized only for those who have submitted to the conditions of the new birth (Jn. 3:3-5), hence, are in Christ's kingdom (Mt. 26:29; Lk. 22:29-30). (d) The supper is to be observed *each* Lord's day. Note the expression *"every* first day of the week" (1 Cor. 16:2 NASB, *et al.*), combined with the *purpose* phrase "to break bread" in Acts 20:7. There is an intimate connection between Christ's death (represented by the elements) and his resurrection (which occurred on Sunday – see Mt. 28:1; Mk. 16:2; Lk. 24:1; Jn. 20:1). Random communion at other times does not have the authority of the Scriptures.

CONFESSION OF FAITH

Paul commended Timothy because the young man had confessed "the good confession" before many witnesses (1 Tim. 6:12). "Confession" is from the Greek *homologia*, literally "to speak the same." The term thus suggests that one must be willing to say regarding Jesus, what the Lord claimed for himself, namely, that he is the Christ, the promised Messiah of the Old Testament, the Son of God, i.e., God in very nature (cf. Mt. 16:16). This commitment to historical reality is absolutely required for salvation (Mt. 10:32; Rom. 10:9-10), and those who refuse to acknowledge the truth regarding the Savior, stand against him (Mt. 12:30; Jn. 12:42-43; 2 Jn. 7). Religious modernists who profess an association with Christianity, yet who deny the fundamental truths regarding his identity, are some of the greatest enemies of the Son of God (cf. Phil. 3:18-19).

CONFESSION OF SINS

As noted above, "confession" means "to say the same thing." In this connection, it is the *personal* acknowledgment of those transgressions in our lives, of which God has spoken, and condemned, by means of divine revelation. But confession involves more than mere tacit acknowledgment. Judas confessed: "I have sinned..." (Mt. 27:4), yet he died lost (Jn. 17:12). Confession must be coupled with repentance, which involves forsaking the sin. When one has sinned against another, or in the presence of another, or simply against God, he must confess it to whatever extent it is known (see Ezra 9:6; Acts 19:18; Jas. 5:16). The dogma of "auricular [in the ear] confession," as taught in Catholic circles (i.e., confessing to a priest), is a practice with no scriptural support. Note that the confession in James 5:16 is reciprocal.

CONSCIENCE

This English term is related to the Latin *conscientia*, literally, "to know together," or "joint knowledge." It corresponds to the Greek *suneidesis* (found thirty times in the N.T.) which essentially has the same meaning. The conscience is an inward faculty, unique to human beings, that either accuses or excuses a person's thoughts, words, and actions (Rom. 2:15). The conscience does not *determine* what is right or wrong (Prov. 14:12; Acts 23:1), but merely judges one, based upon the standard of conduct he has adopted. The conscience must be educated by divine revelation (the Scriptures) and cultivated to remain sensitive to truth (Eph. 4:19; 1 Tim. 4:2; Heb. 5:14). The conscience is such a sensitive instrument that it is wrong to violate it even in matters of expediency (Rom. 14:23). Peter indicates that when one surrenders to the gospel plan of salvation (particularly in the culminating act of baptism), he is appealing to God for a clear conscience (1 Pet. 3:21 ASVfn), which is cleansed ultimately by the blood of Christ (Heb. 9:14).

CONTRADICTION

Critics are fond of charging that the Bible cannot be the word of God because, supposedly, it is characterized by multiple contradictions. Such allegations only reveal that the critic is oblivious to the nature of a *real* contradiction. The Law of Contradiction states: "That a thing should both be, and not be, for the same *object*, at the same *time*, and in the same *sense*, is an impossibility." Let us illustrate each of these components. (a) It is not a contradiction to say: "The ark was carried across the Jordan River," and "The ark was not carried across the Jordan River," if in the first instance one is referring to the "ark of the covenant," while in the other case he alludes to "Noah's ark." (b) It is not a contradiction to suggest that Jesus was *crucified* at the "third hour" (Mk. 15:25), yet he was being *tried* at the "ninth hour" (Jn. 19:14), if the former passage employs *Jewish* time (9:00 a.m.), while the latter is citing *Roman* time (6:00 a.m.). (c) It is not a contradiction for Jesus to affirm that he had a kingdom (Lk. 22:30), and then suggest that he did not have a kingdom – if *his* kingdom was not a this-world kingdom, but rather, was a spiritual regime (see Jn. 18:36). Alleged Bible contradictions can be resolved by the application of these principles if all of the relevant facts are known.

CORINTHIANS 1, BOOK OF

This epistle was written by Paul to a church he had established on his second missionary campaign (Acts 18:1-11). It deals with problems within that local congregation, e.g., division (1:10ff), carnality (3:1ff), immorality (5:1ff) and litigation (6:1ff). Too, it responds to a series of questions that had been sent to Paul reflecting the concerns of the Corinthian saints (7:1ff). There were questions about marriage (7:1ff), meats that had been sacrificed to idols (8:1ff), the support of gospel preachers (9:1ff), conduct in worship (11:1ff), spiritual gifts (12-14), and the bodily resurrection (15).

CORINTHIANS 2, BOOK OF

Paul's second preserved letter to the Corinthian brethren was designed to be corrective in nature. It urged the saints to be forgiving to the brother who had been disciplined because of his fornication (2:1ff; cf. 1 Cor. 5:1ff). It pressed for a correct perspective regarding the law of Moses (3:1ff). It urges the Corinthians to complete a pledged contribution for the needy in Judaea (8-9). Finally, the book also makes a defense of Paul's apostleship in the face of certain radicals who disputed such (10:10; 11:4-15; 12:12; 13:3).

COVENANT

A covenant is an agreement between two parties. In some cases the parties stand on equal footing, and each contributes to the conditions of the covenant. It can be the case, however, that one of the parties is infinitely superior to the other (as in the case of God versus man). Accordingly, the superior (God) has the right to solely dictate the terms of the agreement. The Creator commands; we submit! There are several covenants mentioned in the Scriptures, e.g., God's covenant with Adam and Eve (Gen. 3:15-21), the covenant with Noah (Gen. 6:13-22), etc. But the two *major* covenants of the Bible are: (a) God made a covenant at Sinai with the Israelite nation (Ex. 20:1-24; cf. Dt. 5:1-5). This covenant was *preparatory* in nature and *temporary* in duration; it was abolished by the death of Christ (Rom. 7:4-6; 2 Cor. 3:1ff; Gal. 3:19, 24-25; Eph. 2:14ff; Col. 2:14ff; Heb.

8:7ff). (b) Christ inaugurated a *new* covenant from Jerusalem (see Gal. 4:25), universal in scope (see "many" Mt. 26:28), that was ratified by the shedding of his blood, and is binding until the end of time (cf. Jer. 31:31-34; Heb. 9:15-17). Men today, therefore, are not amenable to the Mosaic code (with its animal sacrifices, physical priesthood, sabbath days, etc.).

CREATION

The creation was the act of an omnipotent God, speaking into existence, from no previous materials, the entire Universe and all that is within it. This concept is unique to Judaic/Christian theology. The doctrine of fiat creation is affirmed in both Testaments (Gen. 1:1-2:25; Psa. 33:9; Jn. 1:1-3; Rom. 1:20; Heb. 11:3), to mention but a fraction of the references. The biblical doctrine of creation is foundational to the balance of the Bible. The creation account, and the immediate events that followed, undergird: (a) The affirmation of man's dignity; he is made in the image of God. (b) The responsibility of humanity – those created, to the Creator (cf. Rom. 9:21); man is required to obey his God. (c) The foundation of the home – the exclusively male/female relationship that constitutes marriage, along with the one-man for one-woman arrangement. (d) The origin and consequences of human sin. (e) The first glimpse of Heaven's plan of redemption (Gen. 3:15). The theory of evolution, concocted by wicked man who desires to be free of divine restraint, proposes another explanation for human existence. Darwinism is a baseless ideology, supported by neither Scripture nor science.

DANIEL, BOOK OF

As a young lad, Daniel was taken into Babylonian captivity along with thousands of others of his people. As a prophetic writer, Daniel's main theme was to emphasize the sovereignty of Jehovah over the nations of the world. He predicted the fall of Babylon and the rise-and-fall of the Medo-Persian, Greek, and Roman empires. He foretells the glorious establishment of God's kingdom in the reign of the Romans, and its permanence in the divine scheme of things (2:44).

DAY

The Hebrew term *yom*, with its Greek equivalent, *hemera*, normally signifies a unit of time determined by the full rotation of the earth upon its axis. That is its meaning in Genesis 1, with reference to the "days" of the creation week. This is made clear by Exodus 20:11, where its import is the same as the sabbath "day." Any attempt to expand the "days" of earth's initial week into eons is a baseless accommodation to evolutionary chronology. In some contexts, however, "day" can take on a figurative meaning, e.g., the "day of salvation" (Isa. 49:8), or the "day of Christ" (Jn. 8:56; cf. 2 Pet. 3:10). It can emphasize a time of urgent opportunity (Jn. 9:4). The final judgment is characterized as a "day" appointed by God (Acts 17:31; Rom. 2:5, 16).

DAY-AGE THEORY

This theory reflects the attempt to accommodate the six days of creation activity (Gen. 1) to the billions of years required by evolutionary chronology. There is overwhelming evidence that the "days" in Genesis 1 are ordinary, solar days. (a) Moses, who wrote the entire Pentateuch, viewed the creation days in the same sense as a sabbath day – obviously, a literal day (Ex. 20:11). (b) The days were equally divided into periods of light and darkness; obviously plants could not survive through "nights" of billions of years. (c) Plants were created the third day; other living creatures were not created until the fifth and sixth days. Plants that are pollinated by insects could never have survived millions of years, awaiting the arrival of insects. (d) Ways of measuring time, e.g., years, months, and days, are determined by heavenly movements. Nothing explains the "week" save the creation span of Genesis 1. (e) In Genesis, "day" (Heb. *yom*), when associated with a definite numeral, indicates a literal day (cf. 7:11; 8:14; 17:12). It is a travesty to twist the Genesis record into conformity with the Darwinian hypothesis.

DEACON

The Greek word *diakonos* comes into the English language as "deacon." The term basically means to serve. It is used of ordinary servants in a secular sense (Jn. 2:5, 9), or of those who serve generally in the cause of Christ (rendered "minister" in 1 Cor. 3:5; 2 Cor. 3:6; Eph. 3:7). It can even be employed of those who serve Satan (2 Cor. 11:15). The word takes on a technical sense, deacons, in some passages (Phil. 1:1). The qualifications for this special work in the church are found in 1 Timothy 3:8-13. *Diakonos* is used of Phoebe in Romans 16:1, though one should not assume that she was a "deaconess" in any official sense. The servants mentioned in Acts 6:1ff may, or may not, have been deacons in a formal way; the evidence is inconclusive.

DEATH

"Death" is a term that, in one sense or another, suggests the idea of *separation.* (a) *Physical* death is that state of the body which is deprived of the "spirit" or "soul" (Gen. 25:8; 35:18; Jas. 2:26). Death is a "mystery" that calls for an explanation. Atheism cannot explain it. If nature has the power to "create" life (as evolutionary dogma asserts), why can it not *sustain* it? The truth is, death is a punishment for man's original rebellion against his Maker (Rom. 5:12). (b) *Spiritual* death is the state of being separated from God by virtue of sin (Isa. 59:1-2; Gen. 2:17; Eph. 2:1, 5; 1 Tim. 5:6). (c) *Eternal* death is the ultimate condition of being forever banished from the presence of God (Rom. 6:23; Rev. 20:14; cf. Mt. 7:23; 2 Thes. 1:7-9).

DEISM

Deism is a religious/philosophical theory that acknowledges the existence of a Supreme Being who was responsible for the creation of the Universe. The transcendent Being, however, has had no direct or indirect interaction with humanity. This philosophy denies, therefore, that Deity came to earth incarnate, in the person of Jesus Christ. Moreover, according to this view, there never have been miracles. God does not hear prayers nor does he operate providentially in today's world. This ideology is a "land of desolation" midway between that of outright atheism, and a fully expressed biblical faith.

DEMONS

Demons (not "devils" KJV) were evil spirits (Mt. 12:43-45) that were permitted to inhabit the bodies of some people during the days of Christ and his apostles. Almost certainly this was for the purpose of allowing the Savior and his men the opportunity of *demonstrating the superiority of God's power* over Satan (see Mt. 12:28-29; Lk. 10:17-18; 1 Jn. 4:4). That power was shown to be effective over nature (Mt. 8:23-27), disease (Mt. 9:20-22), and death (Jn. 11:1-45). Demon-possession, along with the divine authority of expulsion, ceased when the New Testament record was completed and the need for confirmation of divine revelation no longer existed (1 Cor. 13:8ff).

DENOMINATION

A religious body or sect that subscribes to a particular set of doctrinal tenants and is set apart from other religious groups by its name and human creed. Denominations find no divine sanction in the New Testament. They represent a departure from the pristine Christianity of the first century (2 Thes. 2:1ff; 1 Tim. 4:1ff; 2 Tim. 4:1ff). They were historically manifested in the development of Catholicism (Roman and Greek branches), and the subsequent evolution of Protestantism. Over the centuries thousands of sincere people have abandoned the denominations for a return to the apostles' doctrine (Acts 2:42) in both teaching and practice.

DEPRAVITY, TOTAL

The doctrine of hereditary total depravity (known as "original sin" in Roman Catholic circles) is the concept that all children come into the world with both the *effect* and *guilt* of Adam's original sin. By "heredity," therefore, they are totally (completely) depraved (evil), i.e., moral corruption extends to every part of their make-up. Hence, in one's growth towards maturity, before he can believe the gospel, he must be endowed (supernaturally) by the Holy Spirit. This dogma was developed in its earliest and fullest form by Augustine (A.D. 354-430), and later was popularized by John Calvin. It is without biblical evidence. Children do not inherit the sins of their parents (Gen. 8:21; Ezek. 18:20; Mt. 18:1ff; 19:14; 1 Cor. 14:20). Sinning is a matter of choice, not genes (Josh. 24:15; Isa. 7:15). People *go* astray (Isa. 53:6); they are not *born* astray. We are condemned by our *own* sins (Eph. 2:1; ASV), not those of another. [Note: Psalm 51:5 is poetic hyperbole, suggesting that, relatively speaking, the whole of one's life is given to sin (cf. Job 31:18).] See BORN IN SIN.

DESTROY

The Bible occasionally speaks of the wicked being ultimately "destroyed" (*apollumi*) in hell (Mt. 10:28; Lk. 13:3, 5; 2 Thes. 2:10). Some, therefore, have assumed that after an appropriate period of punishment, the spirits of wicked men will be extinguished. But the idea embodied in the word *apollumi* is "ruin, loss of well-being" – not annihilation (W.E. Vine). A sheep was "lost" (*apollumi* - Lk. 15:4, 6), and a wineskin "perished" (*apollumi* – Lk. 5:37), but neither was "out of existence." Nor will the spirits of evil people be extinguished. See ANNIHILATION.

DEUTERONOMY, BOOK OF

This is the fifth book of the Pentateuch. The title signifies "second law." This document was penned by Moses near the end of the era of the wilderness wandering. Its design is to rehearse the law to the new generation that is about to enter

Canaan – the older generation having died out in the wilderness, with the exception of Joshua and Caleb (1:1-3). The book is a reminder to the Hebrew people that they must love God, listen to him, and observe his laws.

DEVIL

The term means to slander, accuse (cf. Rev. 12:9-10). This word is used thirty-three times in the N.T. of the arch-enemy of man, Satan (Mt. 13:28). Since only deity is characterized by underived immortality (1 Tim. 6:16), Satan obviously was created (Col. 1:16). But inasmuch as everything created was judged "very good" (Gen. 1:32), one must conclude that Satan "fell" (cf. 1 Tim. 3:6; 2 Pet. 2:4; Jude 6). His characteristic activity is tempting others to sin ("tempter" in Mt. 4:3 is a present tense participle, indicating sustained action). His temptation of the human family, together with the destruction that has followed, casts him into the role of the "murderer" of mankind (Jn. 8:44; cf. Rom. 5:12). His power over us is limited by our own freewill, so we must resist him (Jas. 4:7; Mt. 26:41), The devil's ultimate destiny is eternal torment in hell (Mt. 25: 41; Rev. 20:10).

DISCIPLINE, CHURCH

Discipline is actually a process of training that begins at the point of one's conversion and continues throughout his life. It includes teaching, example, exhortation, admonition, etc. (2 Tim. 3:16-17). The most extreme and ultimate form of church discipline, however, is the withdrawal of fellowship. This procedure is discussed in several texts (see Mt. 18:15-17; Rom. 16: 17; 1 Cor. 5:1ff; 2 Thes. 3:6, 14-15; Tit. 3:10). Here are some facts gleaned from passages related to this theme: (a) Much love and patient concern must be exhibited in the preliminary stages of the process (Gal. 6:1). (b) Disfellowship must involve a serious, soul-threatening breach of conduct, e.g., immoral activity (1 Cor. 5), divisiveness (Rom. 16:17; Tit. 3:10), etc. It should be a last resort after all other measures of restoration have proved futile (Mt. 18:15-17). (c) The formal act should be exercised in the church assembly (1 Cor. 5:4). (d) Once enacted, common social contacts should be suspended (Mt. 18:17; Rom. 16:17; 1 Cor. 5:9ff; 2 Thes. 3:14-15). (e) Loving encouragement to return to the family should be sustained (cf. Gal. 6:1), and the offender should be happily received upon restoration (2 Cor. 2:6-8).

DISPENSATION

The Greek word *oikonomia* is rendered "dispensation" several times in the N.T. (see 1 Cor. 9:17; Eph. 1:10; 3:2, 9; Col. 1:25). Sometimes the word suggests the idea of managing a household and is rendered as "stewardship" (Lk. 16:2, 3, 4; 1 Cor. 9:17). On other occasions, the word implies a "plan" that has been "arranged" (Eph. 1:10; 3:9). The term may suggest appropriate "training" in divine instruction (1 Tim. 1:4). "Dispensation" is popularly used of a period of time. In Bible parlance, it is commonly used to reference the major eras in which God has operated in implementing the plan of redemption. (a) The *Patriarchal* dispensation extended from the creation of the human family to the commencement of the Mosaic period, at which point God selected the Hebrews as a special people through whom to send Christ (Gen. 12:1ff). In this age, God spoke to man through select prophets. Worship was administered by the father in each family (cf. Job 1). (b) The *Mosaic* dispensation began at Sinai, when Jehovah gave the law of Moses to the Israelite people, thus separating them from the nations of the world as a redemptive tool preliminary to the sending of his Son (Gal. 3:24-25; 4:4). Only the nation of Israel was under this code; the balance of humanity remained under the patriarchal system. The Mosaic religion was terminated at the cross (Col. 2:14ff); it ended in a *political* sense with the destruction of Jerusalem in A.D. 70. (c) The Christian dispensation began on the day of Pentecost and will be terminated at the return of Christ (Isa. 2:2-4; Dan. 2:44; Joel 2:28-30; 1 Cor. 15:24-26), giving way to the eternal order of things.

DISPENSATIONALISM

This is a system of dividing history into seven dispensations, each corresponding to one of the days of the creation week. The theory was popularized by C.I. Scofield in his Reference Bible (1909). These dispensations are alleged to be: Innocence, Conscience, Human Government, Promise, Law, Grace, and Kingdom. Supposedly we are living in the Grace dispensation now, and the Kingdom period will commence when Christ returns to earth to set up his millennial kingdom. This entire theory is a fabrication that contradicts the Scriptures in numerous places. Some elements of this theory, *along with Scripture references that refute them,* are: (a) Christ came to re-establish David's kingdom but *suprisingly* was rejected by the Jews (Psa. 118:22; Isa. 53:1ff). (b) As a result of the Jewish rejection, the kingdom was *postponed* (Mk. 9:1; Mt. 16:19; Col. 1:13; Rev. 1: 6, 9). (c) The church – set up in place of the postponed kingdom – was but an *afterthought* in the mind of God (Eph. 3:10-11). (d) Certain "signs" point to the *imminent* return of Christ (Mt. 24: 34-36; Mt. 25:5). (e) Christ comes to earth *three* times: the first coming in the incarnation; the second coming at the "rapture;" the third coming to begin his "millennial reign" (Heb. 9:28). (f) The Lord's return to earth will *begin* his reign (Lk. 19:15; 1 Cor. 15:24-25). The dispensational doctrine must be rejected.

DIVORCE

Divorce may be defined as the legal dissolution of a marriage covenant. Under the Mosaic regime, divorce could be obtained for a variety of reasons (Dt. 24:1; Mt. 19:8). But this looseness was merely tolerated; it was not the divine ideal. Under the Christian system, the strictness of the marital union was restored to its original design (Mt. 19:8b). Divorce is authorized for one cause only – that of fornication (sexual intercourse) by a marital partner against an innocent victim (Mt. 5:32; 19:9). Mark 10:12 provides the woman with the same right as the man. There may be occasions where the Christian companion may need to separate for safety's sake (cf. 1 Cor. 7:11), but divorce is narrowly permitted. Mere abandonment by a thoughtless spouse does not constitute grounds for divorce and/or remarriage (1 Cor. 7:15).

DOGMA, DOGMATIC

The word "dogma" is not found in the English Bible, but it is in the Greek New Testament. (a) In classical Greek the term had a range of meanings – from "opinion" to a legal "edict." Luke refers to a census "decree" that Augustus sent forth (2:1). This was dogma with the force of law (see also the accusation against Paul in Acts 17:7). (b) The Jerusalem church, under the influence of Spirit-guided men, sent forth certain "decrees" by which other Christians were bound (Acts 16:4; cf. 15:28).

(c) Paul affirmed that the "ordinances" (*dogma*) of the law of Moses had been abolished by the death of Christ (Eph. 2:15; cf. Col. 2:14). (d) The Christian is obligated to sacred dogma, as reflected in the New Testament. He is not required to submit to the humanly devised dogma of fallible man, as conveyed through papal decrees, church councils, etc. One may not be dogmatic in terms of personal opinion; he must be dogmatic in matters of clearly revealed biblical truth.

DRUNKENNESS

Drunkenness involves the ingestion of a mind-altering substance for purely pleasurable purposes. This vice is repeatedly condemned in the Scriptures (Prov. 23:29ff; Eph. 5:18; 1 Cor. 5:11; 6:10; Gal. 5:21). While the Bible does not prohibit the use of certain drugs for medicinal purposes (cf. 1 Tim. 5:23), e.g., codeine or morphine for extreme pain, the dulling of one's mind as an escape from problems that ought to be addressed with spiritual solutions, or for a recreational "high," is not sanctioned in Scripture. It also should be borne in mind that "drunkenness" is a matter of degree. The alteration of one's mental faculties commences almost immediately as one ingests the distilled spirits of our modern world. The Greek word *nepho* (sober) signifies to "be free from the influence of intoxicants" (W.E. Vine). Another factor that must be considered is one's Christian influence (cf. Rom. 14:21). See WINE.

EASTER

The Greek term *pascha* has been mistranslated as "Easter" in the King James Version of the Bible (Acts 12:4). The term is consistently rendered "passover" elsewhere in the N.T. (see Mt.

26:2). The word "Easter" derives from an old Anglo-Saxon term related to the goddess of spring. In the post-apostolic age it was borrowed from paganism and applied to an annual celebration of the Lord's resurrection. There is no N.T. authority for the yearly celebration of "Easter" as a tribute to Christ's resurrection from the dead. Christians honor the Savior's resurrection by worshipping each Sunday as instructed by the Scriptures (Acts 20:7; 1 Cor. 16:1-2).

ECCLESIASTES, BOOK OF

This profound work analyzes the avenues that men commonly explore in the pursuit of temporal happiness. Written by Solomon (1:1) – likely in his advanced years – it affirms that earthly goals, e.g., wealth, power, human wisdom, pleasure, etc., cannot produce true contentment. Man achieves his greatest joy only when he fulfills his purpose in life, namely, demonstrating reverence for his Maker and keeping the divine commandments. Each person will ultimately give account for his choices in life (12:13-14).

ELDER

The Greek term *presbuteros* is rendered "elder." It can refer simply to an older person (cf. Acts 2:17; Heb. 11:2), or it may take on a technical sense – an officer in the church, equivalent to a bishop or pastor. See BISHOP.

ELECT

The English "elect" derives from a compound Greek term, *eklektos* (*ek* – "out of," and *lego* – "to gather"). It suggests the idea of being selected or chosen. It is used in several senses in the N.T. (a) The nation of Israel was elected by God to be the instrument through which Christ would come to earth (Dt. 7:6; Isa. 45:4). (b) Jesus was God's chosen for the implementation of the plan of redemption (1 Pet. 2:4, 6). (c) Angels are elect in that they are used for certain roles in God's providential plan (1 Tim. 5:21). (d) Christians are frequently referred to as God's elect or chosen (Mt. 24:22; Rom. 8:33; Col. 3:12; 2 Tim. 2:10). This does not mean that each child of God was specifically chosen "before the foundation of the world" for salvation, while others were arbitrarily predestined for condemnation – as Calvinism contends. How absurd it is to argue that God commissioned the gospel to be preached to "every creature," when, supposedly, a vast number had been chosen already for eternal damnation! The truth is, God chose a *type* of person, the one who is obedient in disposition, who would *himself* determine to enter the "in Christ" relationship (see Eph. 1:4 "chose us *in him*") by obedience to the truth (Rom. 6:3-4; Gal. 3:26-27). Personal acceptance of the gospel, or thrusting it away, determines who the elect are. A person "judges" *himself* worthy, or unworthy, of eternal life (see Acts 13:46).

EPHESIANS, BOOK OF

This book develops the theme of "God's eternal purpose" (3: 10-11). It reveals that even before the world was formed (1:4), God elected to save a certain type of person (the obedient) on the basis of the merits of his Son's death upon the cross (1:7; 2: 13ff). Salvation is enjoyed within an "in Christ" relationship (this phrase or an equivalent used thirty-five times) . The book exalts the church as the bride of Christ who is submissive to her head (Eph. 5:22ff), and notes that one is sanctified and cleansed by means of receiving the word and being washed with water (baptism) (Eph. 5:25-26).

ESCHATOLOGY

From the Greek word *eschatos* ("last") comes "eschatology," a study of "last things," e.g., the second coming of Christ, the resurrection of the dead, the judgment day, the end of the world, heaven, and hell. In a word, eschatology has to do with the consummation of God's redemptive scheme. The following elements are significant: (a) The Bible teaches that Christ will return (Jn. 14:3; Phil. 3:20; 1 Thes. 4:14ff; 2 Thes. 1:7ff). (b) At the time of his second coming, Jesus will raise all the dead at the same time (Jn. 5:28-29; Acts 24:15). The resurrection of the righteous and the wicked *will not* be separated by a span of 1,000 years – called the millennium, as some allege. (c) There will be a day of judgment upon which all men will give an account for the deeds of their lives (Acts 17:31; Rom. 14:10-12; 2 Cor. 5:10; 2 Tim. 4:1), and God's righteousness will be vindicated (Rom. 2:5). (d) The material world will come to an end (Mt. 24:35; 2 Pet. 3:10ff; Rev. 21:1). (e) The eternal phase of human existence will commence – heaven for the righteous and hell for the wicked (Mt. 25:31ff; v. 46). A bizarre modern theory, called "realized eschatology," argues that each of these forgoing events occurred in A.D. 70 when the Romans demolished the Jewish state. This ideology contradicts Scripture in every particular.

ESTHER, BOOK OF

During that era between the first and second Jewish returns from Babylonian captivity (536 and 457 B.C.), many Hebrews were still in Persia. A dreadful plot to exterminate the Jews was instigated by a Persian official named Haman. Esther, a beautiful Jewess, was raised up by God to be instrumental in the deliverance of her people (Esth. 4:14). She became the queen and, through her influence, Haman was destroyed and the Hebrews were spared. The book also explains the origin of the Jewish feast of Purim, a commemoration of the Jews deliverance from Haman (9-10). An underlying theme is the preservation of the Hebrews in view of the coming Messiah.

ETERNAL LIFE

The concept of eternal life is set forth in an abbreviated format in the O.T. (cf. Dan. 12:2); it comes into full bloom in the revelation of the N.T. Life and immortality are brought to light through the gospel (2 Tim. 1:10). Many entertain the notion that "eternal life," as that glorious promise is set forth in the Bible, is merely eternal *existence.* That is not the case. The wicked will exist forever (Dan. 12:2; Mt. 25:46; Rev. 14:9-12). Eternal life is the opposite of eternal punishment (Mt. 25:46); which is called the "second death" (Rev. 20:14). As noted elsewhere [see DEATH], the "second death" is banishment from the presence of God and everything that is good (Mt. 25:41; 2 Thes. 1:9). Accordingly, "eternal life" is everlasting communion with the wonderful and holy God (knowing him intimately – Jn. 17:3), with his angels, and with the redeemed of the ages (cf. Eccl. 12:7; Lk. 23:43; 2 Cor. 5:8; Phil. 1:23). Eternal life (salvation) is conditioned upon being obedient to Jesus Christ (Heb. 5:8-9).

ETHICS

Ethics has to do with the system or code by which attitudes or actions are determined to be either right or wrong. There are but two possible sources that serve as the bases for ethical conduct; ethical conduct is regulated either by God or man. (a) If ethics derive from God, then he, based upon his own nature, and out of his own sovereignty (see), determines what is right and wrong, and to that standard man submits. This is the biblical position. (b) On the other hand, if ethics originate strictly with man, then each human being is autonomous (see), crafting his own moral code and living as he chooses. Logically, then, he need only avoid such consequential penalties as society may impose. This is a most fallacious system of thought, and no one can live by it ultimately. Every *rational* person will eventually draw the line, with the declaration: "This (outrageous social abuse, e.g., murder, rape, etc.) is wrong!" However, apart from the concept of God, and a divine revelation containing ethical guidelines, there is no consistent defense of a reasonable standard of human behavior. Jesus Christ is the noblest example of ethical conduct that man has ever witnessed.

EVANGELIST

The term "evangelist" is an anglicized form of the Greek *euanglistes*, from *eu* ("well") and *angelos* ("messenger"). It refers to one who proclaims the good message, a gospel herald. In a *generic* sense, all Christians are evangelists. However, the term is used in the N.T. in a more restricted sense – equivalent to a gospel minister (cf. Acts 21:8; Eph. 4:11; 2 Tim. 4:5). In this latter sense, a woman cannot serve as an evangelist (1 Cor. 14:34; 2 Tim. 2:12); in the general sense, she can – and must.

EVOLUTION

A rudimentary form of the theory of evolution was taught by the ancient Greeks. It was popularized in more modern times by the advent of Charles Darwin's book, **The Origin of Species** (1859). It is a rationalistic philosophy that has been invented as a substitute for the biblical record of human origins. The motive is an attempt to escape responsibility to the Creator. As a theory, evolution is bankrupt in terms of explaining: (a) *The Universe*. Matter is neither eternal nor self-created. Evolution cannot explain its existence. (b) *Biological Life*. The law of biogenesis demonstrates that life cannot create itself; evolution cannot explain life. (c) *Design*. Nature tends toward disorder; evolution cannot explain the amazing orderly design in the Universe. (d) *The Origin of Species*. Evolution cannot explain how a one-cell organism could produce the millions of complex creatures upon the earth. (e) *Human Uniqueness*. Evolution cannot explain how raw matter could produce human consciousness, communication, morality, etc. The story of evolution is a work of fantasy for adults who long to be their "own god." See: CREATION.

EXEGESIS

The word means "to lead out." It is a part of the larger *science of interpretation* known as "hermeneutics." A form of the original word is found in John 1:18, where the apostle affirmed that Jesus came to "declare" (*exegeomai*) the Father, i.e., make him known, explain him, be a commentary on God for humanity's sake. To study Christ is, then, in a large measure, to know God (Jn. 14:9). *Biblical exegesis* seeks to bring out the meaning of the sacred text by studying the historical and grammatical features of a passage within its context.

EXISTENTIALISM

Existentialism is the name of a philosophical movement that began in Germany just before World War II. It attempts to probe the meaning of "human existence" apart from divine revelation and the restrictions thereof. It argues that man must never surrender his freedom to a set of rules or a religious code. Rather he must resolve the conflicts of life on his own terms. This decision to find himself, exert himself, and regulate himself – as *his own person* – is, supposedly, the result of God's unconditional acceptance of man. Allegedly this concept enables human beings to have the courage to be themselves. This ideology, which exudes from the very pores of modern society, manifests a total rejection of the authority of the Holy Scriptures. It reflects a vain attempt on the part of rebellious man to do that which is right in his own eyes (Judg. 21:25).

EXODUS, BOOK OF

The name of the second book of the O.T. means "departure" or "going out." It contains Moses' record of Israel's departure from Egyptian bondage and the nation's separation unto God as a holy body of people – in preparation for the coming of the Messiah. Exodus details the giving of the law of Moses to the Hebrew people. It covers about 215 years – from the migration of the Hebrews into Egypt to the reception of the law at Sinai.

EXPEDIENCY

Expediency is sometimes defined as the method by which a determined goal is achieved, regardless of the moral consequences. This is not the *biblical* concept of expediency. In Bible parlance, a method can be expedient only if it is lawful.

If, for example, there is generic authority for a practice, then one may pursue an expedient method of implementing the practice. When Jesus mandated his disciples to evangelize the world (Mt. 28:18-20; Mk. 16:15-16; Lk. 24:46-47), he left it up to them to use the most expedient mode of transportation possible. Sometimes a thing may be lawful, but not expedient (cf. 1 Cor. 10:23). For instance, in apostolic times it was technically lawful to eat meat that had been sacrificed to idols, yet, in some cases (where others might be likely to stumble), it was not expedient (see 1 Cor. 8:1ff; 1 Cor. 10:23ff; Rom. 14).

EZEKIEL, BOOK OF

Ezekiel was a prophet in Babylonian captivity, his ministry lasting more than twenty years. Jeremiah had foretold that the captivity would last seventy years (Jer. 25:11), but false prophets among the captives promised an early return to the homeland. Ezekiel's task was to solemnly warn the Israelites that they must serve the full seventy years. He also condemned certain pagan peoples. Beyond the days of those hardships, however, he looks forward to some of the glories of the Messianic age.

EZRA, BOOK OF

The book documents Israel's first two returns from Babylonian captivity. The time covered in the narrative is about eighty years, from the edict of Cyrus to Ezra's arrival in Jerusalem. The first return was led by Zerubbabel in 536 B.C., and the second was under the leadership of Ezra in 457 B.C. The narrative deals with the rebuilding of the holy city's walls in the aftermath of the horrible destruction of the city by the Babylonians in 586 B.C. Great faith was exhibited and numerous obstacles (e.g., Samaritan opposition) were overcome.

FAITH

Faith is the willingness to trust and obey God without ever having seen him personally. It is not a gullible "leap in the dark," as existential "faith" postulates; rather, it is based upon evidence that allows one to maintain a *prima facie* (self-evident) case for belief. Faith involves believing truth, not myth. Faith is grounded in testimony – the *abstract* testimony of the creation (Psa. 19:1; Rom. 1:20; Heb. 11:1ff), and the *concrete* testimony of Scripture (Rom. 10:17). The term "faith" may be used *subjectively*, i.e., having to do with one's personal faith (Rom. 1:8), or it may be employed *objectively*, i.e., standing for the body of truth (the gospel) revealed to man via inspired spokesmen (Gal. 1:23; 1 Tim. 5:8; Jude 3). Faith that does not express itself in obedience to God is no faith (Gal. 5:6; Jas. 2:14ff). Note how the expression "by faith" is manifested in *action* in Hebrews 11. See also BELIEF.

FAITHFUL

Faithfulness carries the idea of integrity, steadfastness, true, dependable, etc. Two important emphases of this quality are stressed in the Bible. (a) God is faithful in all things (see Psa. 36:5; 100:5; Lam. 3:23). This means one can have absolute confidence in his promises and thus live in marvelous hope. Also, however, it implies that his warnings will not fail. There will be swift and certain retribution for those who flaunt divine grace and the plan through which it is expressed. (b) God demands faithfulness in human beings. The N.T. stresses faithfulness as a quality in Christian people. Christ is our example in this regard (Heb. 2:17; 3:2; Rev. 1:5; 3:14). A number of outstanding Christians are held up in the N.T. as models of faithfulness (see 1 Cor. 4:17; Eph. 6:21; Col. 4:9; 1 Pet. 5:12). Paul affirmed his own fidelity (1 Cor. 7:25; 1 Tim. 1:12). While it is true that the child of God will never reach a plateau of perfection in this life (Phil. 3:12ff), he must strive for faithfulness. Faithfulness is the standard for receiving the "crown of life" (Rev. 2:10). The Calvinistic notion that because "God is faithful," his children can never so stray as to become unfaithful, and thus be lost, is anti-biblical.

FALL, THE

This expression generally refers to the apostasy of Adam and Eve in the garden of Eden, whereby the human family was introduced to heartache, disease, and ultimately death (Gen. 2:17; 3:16ff; Rom. 5:12). Since that awful day, when our race was murdered (Jn. 8:44), we have been a planet in rebellion. The biblical concept of "the fall" is in direct opposition to the evolutionary notion that man has climbed *upward* from a brutish past.

FATHER

God is frequently referred to under the figure of a "father" (107 times in the Gospel of John alone). The Scriptures apply the term in several ways: (a) God is the Father of all men in the sense that he is the Creator of humanity (cf. Mal. 2:10; Ezek. 18:4; Lk. 3:38; Acts 17:28). (b) He is the Father of Jesus Christ (Mt. 3:17; 17:5; Jn. 14:2) in that by his power Jesus was miraculously conceived within the body of a virgin (Lk. 1:35). Christ was not the son of God prior to the incarnation; in that phase of his existence, he was the divine Word (Jn. 1:1ff; see Lk. 1:35, *"shall be called* the son of God"). (c) God is the *spiritual* father of all who, by submitting to the conditions of the "new birth" process (Jn. 3:3-5), become his regenerated children (Tit. 3:5), and a part of his "household" (Eph. 2:19; cf. 1 Tim. 3:15). This relationship occurs in point of fact at the time one is immersed into Christ (Gal. 3:26-27; cf. 4:4-5). See ADOPTION.

FELLOWSHIP

"Fellowship" translates the Greek *koinonia*, meaning "participation, association, sharing," etc. Fellowship exists on two levels – the vertical level (that which the Christian enjoys with God), and the horizontal level (that which children of God share with one another). (a) The Bible stresses the wonderful "communion" that Christians entertain with the entire Godhead. We fellowship with the Father as we live in harmony with his will (1 Jn. 1:3; 1 Cor. 1:9). We particularly enjoy fellowship with Christ when we observe the "communion" supper (1 Cor. 10:16). There is even a communion with the Holy Spirit (2 Cor. 13:14). (b) There also is the fellowship that believers share with each other (1 Jn. 1:3). Such fellowship can only be enjoyed, however, with those who are sincerely seeking to "walk in the light" of divine truth (1 Jn. 1:7). When a child of God becomes rebellious and unreachable by any other means, fellowship with him must be terminated, to the end that he will feel the isolation and return to the warmth of his spiritual family (2 Thes. 3:6; 14-15). See DISCIPLINE, CHURCH. One final comment. The Christian is not to fellowship (participate in) the "unfruitful works of darkness, but rather reprove them" (Eph. 5:11). This does not mean, however, than he can have no association at all with those in the world – for then he would have to leave the world (1 Cor. 5:9ff), and he could exert no influence for good (Mt. 5:14-16). One must never, however, *share activity* in an evil work.

FIRST DAY OF THE WEEK

This phrase appears eight times in the N.T. It is the ancient expression for what modern society calls "Sunday." The significance of this day can be readily seen in the following cases: (a) It was the day upon which Christ was raised from the dead (Mt. 28:1; Mk. 16:2, 9; Lk. 24:1; Jn. 20:1). (b) The Lord's day was the day upon which the kingdom of Christ was established (Acts 2:1; cf. Lev. 23:15-16). (c) It was the day upon which the church assembled to observe the Lord's supper (Acts 20:7). (d) Sunday was the day the church regularly met to give into the treasury of the congregation for benevolent and evangelistic purposes (1 Cor. 16:1-2). In this passage, the Greek text specifically says, "upon the first day of every [*kata*] week." Though the early disciples frequently entered Jewish synagogues on the sabbath day, in order to teach the Hebrew people, there is no evidence at all in the N.T. that the early Christians (even Jewish Christians) *worshipped* on the sabbath day. The sabbath, along with other elements of the Mosaic law, was abrogated at the cross (Col. 2:14ff).

FIRSTFRUITS

Each year the ancient Hebrews would offer the "firstfruits" of their crops to God as a token of their thanksgiving for the bounty that would follow (Lev. 2:12, 23; 23:17, 39). Borrowing from this circumstance, in his initial letter to the saints at Corinth, Paul refers to Jesus as the "firstfruits" of them who are asleep (1 Cor. 15:20, 23). The imagery affirms that Jesus' resurrection from the dead is *God's pledge* to us that we too shall be raised from the grave at the time of the Lord's return. This argument was designed to rebut the claim of some at Corinth who argued there would be no resurrection (1 Cor. 15:12). It effectively refutes those today who teach the same heresy. See ESCHATOLOGY.

FIRSTBORN

In the O.T., this term referred to the *first* individual born to parents, whether of man or beast. The firstborn was accorded a place of special prominence (cf. Gen. 48:13-18; Dt. 21:15-17; 2 Chron. 21:3). The word also came to be used in a figurative sense. The "firstborn" of death signified an especially deadly disease (Job 18:13), and "firstborn" of the poor meant "poorest of the poor" (Isa. 14:30). In the N.T., when the church is designated as a congregation of "firstborn [ones]" (Heb. 12:23), the design is to stress the glorious, exalted position of the people of God. Some have grossly misunderstood the descriptive used of Christ, "the firstborn of all creation" (Col. 1:15). The "Jehovah's Witnesses" allege that this term suggests that Jesus was the first creature created by Jehovah at the beginning of time. Such a view not only contradicts passages which affirm the eternality of the Second Person of the Godhead (e.g., Mic. 5:2; Jn. 1:1; 8:58, Rev. 22:13, etc.), it also fails to recognize the meaning of "firstborn" in context. The "Firstborn" of creation (1:15) no more means that Christ was the *first* created being, any more than "firstborn" from the dead suggests he was the *first* one ever raised from the dead (1:18). In both cases, the idea of *preeminence* is being emphasized. Note the qualifying phrase in 18b, "...that in all things he might have the preeminence."

FLOOD

The Flood, recorded in Genesis 6-8, was the most widespread disaster ever to effect this planet. Waters from the atmosphere above, and from chasms beneath the earth, inundated the entire globe (Gen. 7:19, 21; cf. 2 Pet. 3:6). More than 200 traditions of an ancient, universal flood, from which only a few people were saved, are found among the various nations of the earth. The Flood is significant from several vantage points. (a) The Flood is the best explanation of the fossil record (millions of fossils being found, wildly buried together), as opposed to the evolutionary theory of geology (gradualism). (b) It reflects a graphic example of God's displeasure with human rebellion; it was a judgment against a corrupt antique world (Gen. 6:5, 7, 13; Lk. 17:26-27; 1 Pet. 3:20). (c) The Flood's alteration of Earth's geophysical features provides a partial explanation for the great disasters (earthquakes, hurricanes, etc.) that plague man yet today. This is a part of the price of human rebellion. (d) The Flood narrative presents a "type" (symbolic picture) of our salvation. As Noah and his family were delivered from the corruption of a godless environment by means of water, so similarly, we are moved from a domain of evil (called "the world" – Col. 1:13) to an "in Christ" relationship, by means of the requirement of baptism (1 Pet. 3:20-21). (e) The evidence of the Flood is a perpetual warning of universal judgment that awaits this planet at the time of Christ's return (Mt. 24:37-39; 2 Pet. 3:1ff).

FOREKNOWLEDGE

The Bible affirms the omniscience of God, i.e., the fact that he knows everything – past, present, and future (1 Sam. 16:7; Psa. 139; Isa. 40:13ff; Acts 1:24; Heb. 4:13). One aspect of divine omniscience is "foreknowledge" (*prognosis* – knowing beforehand), an attribute affirmed of God in Acts 2:23 and 1 Peter 1:2. A verbal form of the term is also found in Romams 8:29; 11:2. God has always known everything that will ever happen. The Lord's foreknowledge, as reflected in prophecy, is one of the major evidences of the Bible's divine origin. Foreknowledge, however, does not imply *causation*. The fact that Jehovah knows man's future conduct does not mean that he directs that activity. Were that the case, no one would ever be personally responsible for his own actions – which is contrary to the explicit testimony of Scripture (Rom. 14:12; 2 Cor. 5:10). God foreknew the death of Christ (Acts 2:23), but those who perpetrated the horrible deed were responsible for their transgression (2:36-38). Moreover, if God's foreknowledge of events implies that he orchestrates them, and man is thus robbed of his free will, then every command to man in the Bible is meaningless, for the person could not do otherwise but to obey or disobey. The Calvinistic theory of divine "foreknowledge" is an egregious reflection upon the character of the Creator. See ELECT.

FORGIVENESS

The most common word in the Greek N.T. which conveys the idea of "forgiveness" is *aphesis*, a compound term meaning "to send away from." (a) Forgiveness is a divine response to human sin, issuing out of the loving and merciful disposition of God (Jn. 3:16; Eph. 2:4). Forgiveness is possible on the basis of Christ's death – an innocent victim satisfying the demands of divine justice (Isa. 53:11; Rom. 3:21ff). But forgiveness is extended only to those who submit to God's plan for pardon (Mk. 16:16; Acts 2:38; 22:16; 1 Pet. 3:21). Man's obedience merits nothing (Eph. 2:8-9). Forgiveness is neither deserved nor earned (Mt. 18:21ff); it is, however, conditional (Heb. 5: 8-9). (b) The spirit of forgiveness must obtain also among men. Though no man has the absolute power to forgive sins (see Mk. 2:7) – Roman Catholic claims to the contrary notwithstanding – we must always cultivate the *merciful spirit*, willing to extend pardon to any penitent transgressor (Lk. 17:3). Judgment will be without mercy to him who shows no mercy (Jas. 2:13; cf. Mt. 6:12; 18:32-35).

FORM CRITICISM

Form Criticism is a modern approach to the Bible that has its origin in a liberal mentality. It asserts, for example, that the Gospel records are basically "myths." The "scholarly critic," therefore, must probe behind the written accounts, and their "literary sources," in an effort to find the oral traditions that underlie them. The method then proposes to classify the traditions according to certain story-types. R.C. Foster has noted that form criticism is "fundamentally an attack upon the historical verity of the New Testament documents." He charges that the theory assumes that the Gospel writers did not have enough "native intelligence" to observe and ascertain with assurance the events of which they wrote, and then to write them down in a clear format that is historically reliable. The leading proponents of form criticism are hopelessly in contradiction with one another. There is no reason not to accept the Gospel accounts as the *inspired writings* of men who were chosen by the Lord to record the essential details of his earthly sojourn. Whatever sources may have been employed (cf. Lk. 1:1-4), the writers' composition of the documents most assuredly was under the guidance of the Spirit of God (2 Tim. 3:16-17).

FORNICATION

The Greek term *porne* is a comprehensive term, covering *every sort* of illicit sexual activity by human beings. Note: (a) Unmarried people who desire to vent their sexual appetites may marry; otherwise, such activity is "fornication" (1 Cor. 7:2). (b) The married person who has sexual relations with someone other than his/her spouse, in addition to committing adultery, has committed fornication – the latter term embracing the former (Mt. 5:32; 19:9). Jesus taught that the only valid reason for a divorce, and subsequent remarriage, is when one marriage partner commits fornication against his/her innocent victim. (c) Homosexual conduct is also fornication, as Jude 7 clearly indicates. The rebellious fornicator is subject to disciplinary action by the church (1 Cor. 5), and those who persist in this sin cannot enter heaven (1 Cor. 6:9-10). Sometimes the term "fornication" is used symbolically to denote apostasy from the faith (Rev. 17:2; 19:2).

FREE WILL

Animals operate largely according to instinct, an inherited pattern of behavior. Human beings are different. Made in the very image of God himself (Gen. 1:26-27), people possess volition, i.e., the power to make personal choices. A few modern philosophers, like Bertrand Russell, denied that man has free will. Some theologians, following Augustine, contend that man's enslavement to sin has destroyed his power to exercise free will. Accordingly, he can do *nothing* good, not even believe in God, until and unless he is supernaturally empowered with a measure of the Holy Spirit. But this is a false ideology. Every command issued to man presupposes his ability either to accept or reject it. Every warning in Scripture assumes that human beings have the power to change. Jesus said to certain Jews who were rejecting him, "you *will not* come unto me that you may have life" (Jn. 5:39; cf. Mt. 23:37). There is a vast difference between "will not" and "cannot." The canon of Scripture virtually closes with an affirmation of man's free will: "…he that *will*, let him take the water of life freely" (Rev. 22:17).

FULNESS OF TIME

This phrase is found in Galatians 4:4, where Paul speaks of Christ's birth and earthly ministry as occurring when "the fulness of time" had arrived. The expression takes note of the preparation that God, across the centuries, had providentially worked out, so as to ensure the success of the commencement of Christianity. For example: (a) The Hebrew people had given the ancient world a monotheistic religion and a body of inspired Scripture, announcing the coming of the Messiah. (b) The Greeks provided the *Koine* Greek language, the most perfect instrument for the conveyance of human thought ever known to man. (c) The Romans contributed a marvelous system of law (under which Jesus was declared "innocent" of any wrongdoing – see Acts 2:23), as well as a remarkable highway system which facilitated the distribution of the gospel. Everything came together with pinpoint focus; truly, God was the master planner who brought it to glorious fruition.

GALATIANS, BOOK OF

A Jewish element in the church taught that one must be obedient to the law of Moses, as well as to the Gospel, in order to be saved. This book refutes that idea. There are three main elements to Paul's argument to the Galatian churches. First, there is a defense of his apostleship, thus, his authority (1-2). Second, there is the proposition that the law served a temporal, preparatory function; it was abolished, therefore, by the completion of Christ's mission (3-4). Finally, one must personally accept his responsibility to avoid the works of the flesh and to pursue the development of the Spirit's fruit (5-6).

GAMBLING

Gambling may be defined as the willingness to take a risk (a wager), motivated by the desire to get something for nothing. Gambling, an ancient vice condemned in virtually all societies, is motivated by the desire for *gain*, a lust for *excitement*, and the passion for *combativeness*. To express the matter from another angle, gambling is fuelled by *covetousness*, *laziness*, and *recklessness*. Gambling: (a) Violates the principle of responsible stewardship (1 Cor. 4:2; Lk. 16:2). (b) It ignores the concept of the "Golden Rule," seeking to take money from others without the exchange of any service (Mt. 7:12; cf. 22:39). (c) Gambling tends toward addiction; there is even a Gamblers Anonymous (cf. 1 Cor. 6:12). (d) This vice has a sordid historical reputation and tarnishes the Christian's influence (cf. Rom. 12:17; 1 Tim. 5:14). (e) Gambling bears bitter fruit; it frequently leads to massive debts, stealing and the like – to cover losses. It can lead to poverty, divorce, and even suicide (Mt. 7:16). The sincere child of God should refrain from gambling in any form and to any degree.

GAP THEORY

This is the erroneous theory that a vast span of time (billions of years) transpired between Genesis 1:1 and 1:2. During this time period, huge creatures roamed the earth (e.g., dinosaurs), and there was a satanic rebellion among a pre-adam race of men. This revolt precipitated a massive destruction, evidence of which, supposedly, is found in the fossil record. This is a fantasy theory with no factual basis. It clearly contradicts other biblical passages (see Ex. 20:11; 1 Cor. 15:45; Gen. 1:31; 3:20; Rom. 5:12). This notion became popular in the early 1800's in an attempt to bring the Genesis narrative into harmony with evolutionary theories (requiring enormous periods of time), which asserted that our planet is billions of years in age. This view is a compromise ploy unworthy of serious consideration. It is at variance with both Scripture and science.

GENEALOGY

A genealogy is a registry of names of the ancestors or descendants of a particular people. A number of genealogical lists are recorded in the Bible – for example in Genesis, Chronicles, Matthew, and Luke. These are not mere meaningless, boring lists of names. Rather they served important functions. (a) These catalogs show the history of mankind – back to Adam, providing some information about the development of the major nations of the world. (b) Genealogies trace the history of the nation of Israel, and establish, therefore, the lineage of the Messiah. They have an evidential value. (c) They were important in establishing property rights, especially in the post-captivity period. (d) Genealogies provided the information for tribal heritage, so vital in establishing the lineages of the priesthood and the royal line. (e) The genealogies, together with some accompanying chronologies (Gen. 5, 11), demonstrate that mankind has been upon the earth only a few thousand of years (not several million, as evolutionary dogma asserts). The "gaps" in some genealogies are minor, and apparently are mostly filled-in by parallel records. Since humanity came into existence during the same week as the Universe (Gen. 1; Ex. 20:11; Mk. 10:6; Rom. 1:20), this provides evidence of the "youth" of our Universe. There is no solid proof in science that contradicts the "young earth" view.

GENESIS

The opening book of the Bible is a document of "beginnings." Written by Moses some 1,500 years before Christ, it introduces the beginning of: the Universe, life, mankind, the home, sin, the plan of redemption, nations, diverse human languages, and the Hebrew family – through whom the Savior would enter the world. It spans that era of time from the creation to the death of Joseph.

GIFT

The Bible is filled with affirmations of the generosity of our Creator. Every good and perfect gift is from him (Jas. 1:17). Surely our gratitude must be lavishly expressed for his graciousness. (a) God has given us life itself (Acts 17:25; 1 Tim. 6:13). Human life, therefore, is sacred. (b) Jehovah gives us daily provisions that we could not enjoy but by his favor (Acts 14:17; cf. Mt. 6:11). (c) Salvation, by means of Christ's death (Jn. 3:16), is God's gift to humanity (Rom. 6:23; Eph. 2:8-9). (d) The Holy Spirit is given to those who obey the gospel (Acts 2:38; cf. Rom. 8:26). Many erroneously believe, however, that when an object is a *gift*, there can be no conditions attached. If there were, they argue, such would nullify the gift. That conclusion is not correct. Though "life" is a gift, we must sustain it by conforming to the laws of nature. Though our daily bread is God's gift, if we fail to sow and harvest, we will starve. Similarly, though salvation is a "free gift" (Rom. 6:23), and cannot be "earned" like "wages," nonetheless, being "delivered" from sin only occurs when one has been "obedient from the heart" to the correct "form of teaching" (Rom. 6:17). The same context informs us that this occurs when one is "raised" from the grave of "baptism" to walk in "newness of life" (6:3-4). Jesus plainly admonished that one must "*work for* ... eternal life," which, he added, "the Son of man shall *give* unto you" (Jn. 6:27). Man's obedience does not cancel God's generosity. And no gift, however lovingly given, can ever be utilized until it is "received" (cf. Jn. 1:12).

GIVING

Some seventeen different words are found in the Greek N.T. that represent, in one way or another, the concept of "giving." (a) While God does not "need" anything from man (Acts 17:25), he has always demanded that those who wish to serve him should give of their resources for the welfare of others in a variety of prescribed ways (see TITHE). (b) Frequently "giving" is viewed as an overture of worship (Num. 18:11; cf. Heb. 5:1; Mt. 2:11; Phil. 4:18). (c) Since giving is a form of worship, and inasmuch as worship must be according to truth (Jn. 4:24; 17:17), it is clear that the Christian is not without direction in the obligation to give of his income. Some basic facts regarding giving, as gleaned from 1 Corinthians 16:1-2, are as follows: (a) Giving is the duty of "each" Christian who has prospered. (b) Giving is to be "upon the first day of *every week*" (Greek text). (c) It is to be into the "store" (treasury) of the local church. (d) The amount must be commensurate with one's prosperity. While the foregoing is required as a Lord's day feature of worship, Christians are at liberty to give at other times as they have opportunity (Mk. 14:7; Gal. 6:10).

GOD

"God" (*theos*) is the name of the divine *nature*. "God" simply signifies the essence of being deity. Important facts regarding the Deity are these: (a) There is *one* God (Dt. 6:4; Jas. 2:19), i.e., a unified divine nature consisting of the sum total of those qualities that distinguish a Being as divine. Some of the non-moral traits of deity are: eternality, omnipotence, omniscience, omnipresence, etc. Moral qualities of God include: holiness, love, benevolence, justice, mercy, etc. (b) The divine nature is possessed by three distinct personalities, revealed in the N.T. as Father, Son, and Holy Spirit. The Father is God (Eph. 1:3), as is the Son (Jn. 1:1; 20:28; Heb. 1:8), and the Holy Spirit as well (Acts 5:3-4). Though God may not be demonstrated physically, as in a scientific method, nonetheless, a *prima facie* case for his existence is so overwhelming that only the fool denies it (Psa. 14:1; Rom. 1:20ff). See ATHEISM. God's existence may be argued logically on the basis of: (a) *Cause/Effect*. God is the only adequate cause to explain the Universe. (b) *Design/Designer*. The intricate order/design of the Universe demands a Designer, thus, an Intelligence, which, in turn implies Personality. (c) *Moral Sense/Moral Ruler*. The moral sensitivity of the human family suggests an ultimate moral Source by which right and wrong are measured. As atheist Jean Paul Sartre conceded: "If there is no God, nothing is wrong."

GODS

The gods of the biblical era were profuse. They were the inventions of the human mind in a world that had rejected the true God and his sovereignty over humanity. The O.T. prophets denied the reality of pagan gods (cf. Jer. 2:28), as did the N.T. writers (1 Cor. 8:4). Nevertheless, the Lord's people were ever tempted to worship false gods, e.g., Baal, Molech, etc. (cf. Ezek. 16), though the law of Moses explicitly forbade such (Ex. 20:3-6). Because of the sin of idolatry, the kingdom of Israel was taken into Assyrian captivity (722-21 B.C.), and the kingdom of Judah was carried into Babylon, beginning in 606 B.C. – for a span of seventy years. Upon their return from Babylon, the Hebrew people never worshipped idols again – though they were afflicted with numerous other lapses in fidelity. The Scriptures warn that any object can be elevated to the status of a "god," when one's service to Jehovah is subordinated to interests that are deemed to be more important (cf. Col. 3:5; Mt. 6:33).

GOOD

"Good" in the Bible is expressed in a variety of ways. It can have reference to that which is perfect in design, flawless. Such was the state of the earth at the conclusion of the creation week (Gen. 1:30), which, incidentally, reveals that there was no destructive catastrophe in an alleged "gap period" between Genesis 1:1 and 1:2. See GAP THEORY. Eventually, though, "good" came to take on an ethical sense. Though the ancient Greeks spoke of "the good," their concept was far beneath the biblical view. "Good," in Bible parlance, is that which conforms to the character of God. God is good, and if man would partake of that quality, he will keep the divine commands (cf. Mt. 19:

17; cf. 1 Pet. 1:15). Heaven's "goodness" is seen at its clearest in the unfolding of the scheme of redemption (cf. Tit. 3:4-7). The concept of "goodness" exists only with human beings, and this is evidence of the vast chasm that exists between man and other forms of biological life. This is a problem for evolutionists; how can "good" evolve from mere matter?

GOSPEL

"Gospel" derives from the Greek *euangelion*, literally "good tidings" (see Lk. 2:10 where it is fully translated). The gospel (mentioned more than 75 times in the N.T.) is the good news of a plan of redemption for fallen man. Much can be learned about the gospel by a consideration of certain phrases used with the term. (a) It is the "gospel of God" (Mk. 1:14) because it reflects the Father's eternal plan (Eph. 3:10-11). (b) It is the "gospel of Christ," (Mk. 1:1), being focused upon the Lord's mission, and validated by his death. (c) It is the "gospel of grace" (Acts 20:24) because man is undeserving of it. (d) It is the "gospel of salvation" (Eph. 1:13) because salvation is obtained only by obedience to its commands. (e) It is the "gospel of peace" (Eph. 6:15) because obedience to the commands of the system brings peace with God. (f) It is the "gospel of the kingdom" (Mt. 4:23) because in submitting to it we enter the kingdom of Christ. This gospel must be preached (Mk. 16:15), believed (Mk. 1:15), obeyed (2 Thes. 1:8; 1 Pet. 4:17), and defended (Phil. 1:16). Moreover, the Christian must live so as to cause no hindrance to the gospel (1 Cor. 9:12).

GRACE

The term "grace" occurs about 155 times in the N.T. The word relates to a Greek term, *chairo*, meaning "to rejoice," and grace itself comes to mean favor, gratification, or gratitude – depending upon the context. There is great N.T. stress upon the fact that salvation is the result of God's grace (Eph. 2:8-9), but there are several important aspects to this matter. (a) Heaven's grace is made available to "all men" (Tit. 2:11), contrary to the claims of Calvinism, which alleges that it is bestowed only upon certain "elect" ones. (b) Divine grace is accessed by means of a system of intellectual instruction (Tit. 2:12; cf. Jn. 6:45); it is not arbitrarily bestowed. (c) Grace is not extended unconditionally (cf. Gen. 6:8; Heb. 11:7) – again, *contra* Calvinism. The Ephesian Christians had been saved "by grace" (Eph. 2:8), but the salvation occurred at that point in time when they were "cleansed by the washing of water" (Eph. 5:26). (d) Grace excludes merit; salvation can never be earned (Rom. 6:23; cf. Mt. 18:24-27), but grace must be accessed (Rom. 5:2). (e) By grace we can be at peace with God (Rom. 5:1-2), and achieving that, we become heirs of "the grace of life" (1 Pet. 3:7). (f) But it is imperative that the child of God "continue in the grace" he has received (Acts 13:43), and "grow" therein (2 Pet. 3:18). If we do not, we will "fall away" from divine grace (Gal. 5:4; cf. Heb. 12:5), and the grace previously received will have been "in vain" (2 Cor. 6:1 cf. 1 Cor. 15:10).

GREEK

The New Testament was written originally in what is known as *Koine* Greek. *Koine* is to be distinguished from *Attic* Greek, the latter being predominately the language of the ancient classics, e.g., Aristotle, Herodotus, etc. Nor is the Greek of the

N.T. equivalent to the language of modern Greece. The *Koine* period extended from about 330 B.C. to A.D. 330 – at which point it became a "dead" language, undergoing no further significant changes. *Koine* means "common," and this was the period of "common" or "universal" Greek. The conquests of Alexander the Great spread the Greek language far and wide. The Old Testament was translated into *Koine* in the third century B.C. (a version known as the Septuagint - abbreviated as LXX). Much has been learned over the past century about this language; it was the language of the man-on-the-street, the communication of correspondence, contracts, etc. It is a vivid language, containing a variety of tenses (expressing different kinds of action) and prepositions (both as isolated words and as adjuncts to other forms). *Koine* Greek was the most precise instrument for expressing human thought in the history of languages. It is little wonder that God chose it to convey the most important document of all time – the New Testament of our Lord and Savior, Jesus Christ. See FULNESS OF TIME.

HABAKKUK, BOOK OF

Sometime before the fall of Jerusalem to the Babylonians (586 B.C.), the prophet Habakkuk wonders why God appears to have ignored Judah's sins. The Lord informs the bewildered prophet that he is planning punishment for the nation – the Chaldeans (Babylonians) are coming. Habakkuk complains that the Chaldeans are a brutal and evil people – worse even than Judah. Never mind. Babylon will be judged too – eventually. The prophet appears to understand, and he praises Jehovah for his marvelous operations in history. God's people must learn to trust him and wait for the consummation of his plan.

HADES

This word comes directly from Greek into English. W.E. Vine noted that some derive the term from the negative prefix *a* ("not") and *eido* ("seen"), hence "the unseen," though he felt the more likely possibility is that it comes from *hado*, signifying "all receiving." In the KJV it is rendered "hell," but this is incorrect. Hades is the generic name for the intermediate state of the dead, i.e., the receptacle of the soul – whether pertaining to the righteous or the wicked. Jesus was in Hades while his body resided in the tomb (Acts 2:27). Likewise, the selfish rich man, mentioned by Christ, was tormented in his Hadean abode (Lk. 16:23). At the time of Christ's return, when all bodies are raised from the dead (Jn. 5:28-29; Acts 24:15), Hades will surrender the spirits it has retained (Rev. 1:18; 20:13-14). Then, both the good people and the bad will enter their final destinies, with bodies (incorruptible in nature – 1 Cor. 15:53-54) and souls reunited (Mt. 10:28; 2 Cor. 5:1ff).

HAGGAI, BOOK OF

After Judah's initial return from Babylonian captivity (536 B.C.), God's people had begun the work of rebuilding the temple. Then, due to opposition from certain enemies, the Hebrews became discouraged, and the labor ceased. Haggai rebuked his people because they built their own fine homes, and yet allowed the house of God to "lie waste" (1:4). The prophet also swept their minds forward to the time of Christ when Jehovah's house would be characterized by an even greater glory, and peace (of a *spiritual* nature) would prevail (2:6ff).

HEALING

By virtue of man's transgression, death and all its attendant evils (sicknesses) have become a part of the human experience. It is not surprising, therefore, that "healing" is a biblical theme. Healing is spoken of in several senses in Scripture. (a) In the inspired Scriptures, many regulations and principles were designed to promote healing in a *natural* way. The law of Moses has been called "a model of sanitary and hygienic insight." It contains dietary laws, procedures for isolation from infections, etc. (cf. Dt. 23:12-13). The Bible encourages mental attitudes that facilitate healing (Psa. 42:11; Prov. 16:24; Jer. 30:12-17). God wants us to be healthy in body and soul (3 Jn. 2). (b) During those special times when Jehovah was using miracles as a confirmation method in connection with the revelation of divine truth, healing was effected supernaturally. Jesus healed blindness (Jn. 9:1ff), deafness (Mk. 7:31-37), hemorrhaging (Lk. 8:43-48), leprosy (Lk. 17:11-19), and numerous other maladies. Supernatural healing, however, like other miracles, was a temporary phenomenon (see 1 Cor. 13:8ff), and one cannot expect such signs in the modern world. See MIRACLES. (c) There is also the process of healing as a part of the body's marvelous design (Psa. 139:14). Even skeptics have marveled at the ability of the human body to heal wounds and fight disease. Dr. William Beck of Harvard, in a book titled **Human Design**, described wound healing as "among the most complex and interesting self-regulating processes in physiology." The body's immune system, and the work of antibodies, absolutely defy understanding to this very day. (d) The Bible uses the term "healing" of spiritual sicknesses as well. Jesus spoke of the hardness of heart characteristic of the Jewish leaders of his day; yet they would not come to him for soul healing (Mt. 13:15; Jn. 12;40; cf. Heb. 12:13). It is by means of Christ's atoning death that one is "healed" from the disease of sin (Isa. 53:5; 1 Pet. 2:24). How desperately we need the healing of the Great Physician (Lk. 5:30-32).

HEART

The Greek word for "heart" is *kardia* (as in the English, cardiac). Though "heart" *literally* refers to the blood pump within man's body cavity, the term rarely refers to the physical organ in the Bible (yet see 2 Sam. 18:14). "Heart" is used, therefore, mainly in a figurative sense in the Scriptures. The term depicts certain types of dispositions – for good or evil. (a) Solomon once wrote of the one who has the "prudent heart" which, as he subsequently explains, represents the one who seeks knowledge (Prov. 18:15). Some have a thirst for truth and will search for it (cf. Acts 17:11). (b) In one of his parables, Jesus spoke of those who possess the "honest and good heart," i.e., they have an aura of sincerity about them – a willingness to learn and obey. (c) The Lord once rebuked the Jewish leaders of his day, because they were not interested in seeing, hearing, or "understand[ing] with [their] hearts" (Mt. 13:10ff). With some religions, "understanding" is unimportant, because factual history is irrelevant. With Christianity, that is not the case. The religion of Jesus is intellectual as well as emotional. (d) One may be exposed to the truth, and even understand its basic elements, and yet not be inclined to obey it. It is imperative, therefore, that one cultivate the "obedient heart" (cf. Rom. 6:17). (e) Once one has become a Christian, he must grow, and guard himself against "sliding" back into his old ways. Scripture speaks of those who develop the "backsliding" heart (Prov. 14:14). More than a dozen times, Jeremiah warned the nation of Israel about backsliding (cf. Jer. 3:22), and Hosea called the northern kingdom a "backsliding heifer" (4:16). These admonitions contradict the denominational notion that a child of God cannot be lost (cf. Heb. 3:12). See APOSTASY. (f) Pharaoh of Egypt is an example of one who so resisted God that his heart became "hardened" (Ex. 8:15, 32; 9:34; 13:15). And while it is also true that *Jehovah* hardened his heart, such language merely expresses the "permissive" will of God, i.e., Jehovah made demands upon the king that he refused to obey, and the Lord allowed him to grow in stubbornness until a time of reckoning was reached. The Christian must guard his own heart against becoming hard and insensitive (cf. 1 Tim. 4:1ff; Eph. 4:19).

HEAVEN

The term "heaven" is used in different ways in the Bible. (a) The expression may refer to the atmospheric region just above the earth wherein the birds fly, the rain is formed, and in which the wind blows (Gen. 1:10; 7:11; Dan. 8:8). (b) The outer space region that houses the stars, the sun, and the planets is also designated as "heaven" or the "heavens" (Gen. 1:14; 15:5; Isa. 13:10). Both of these above-us material regions will be destroyed at the time of the Lord's return (Mt. 24:35; 2 Pet. 3:7ff; Rev. 21:1). (c) The abode of God is also designated as "heaven" (Psa. 11:4; Mt. 5: 16; 6:9), though the focus of his presence there must not be viewed in a way so as to negate the concept of his presence everywhere (Jer. 23:24). This spiritual region is also known as the "heaven of heavens" (Dt. 10:14; Psa. 115:16), or "the third heaven" (2 Cor. 12:2). This glorious place (Jn. 14:2) will be the final reward of all the faithful (Col. 1:5; 1 Pet. 1:4). Heaven, for the saints, will involve many things. It will be a wonderful place of *rest* (Heb. 4:11; Rev. 14:13), in which we will *reap* the rewards of earthly labors (Gal. 6:9; Mt. 6:19; Lk. 16:9; 1 Cor. 3:14). Heaven will be an environment of great *rejoicing* for the victory won (Mt. 25:21; Rev. 12:11-12; 19:7). It will be a realm of *responsibility* – a further state of service to God (Rev. 22:3; Lk. 19:16-19). Heaven also will involve precious *reunions* of the faithful (Gen. 25:8; 35:29; 37:35; 2 Sam. 12:23; Mt. 8:11; 1 Thes. 2:19-20). Surely the Christian must dedicate himself so as not to miss this ultimate glory. (d) Finally, the term "heaven" is sometimes used figuratively for God himself (Mk. 11:30; Lk. 15:18, 21).

HEAVENS, NEW

On several occasions the Scriptures speak of a "new heavens and a new earth" (2 Pet. 3:13; Rev. 21:1). What does the phrase mean? (a) It does not refer to a *literal* new heavens and earth. This is so very obvious in that these very contexts speak of the material heavens and earth being destroyed, passing away, and existing "no more." (b) The "new heavens and new earth" becomes a *figure of speech* signifying a new environment. Just as we now live in an environment in which we breathe the air of "heaven," and take sustenance of the bounties of the "earth," even so, we look forward to a future realm, not material in nature, but a "new heavens and new earth" of *spiritual* composition. Simple logic establishes this conclusion. In logic there is a principle which suggests that things equal to each other are equal to the same thing. If it is the case that "heaven" is our eternal home (and it is – see above), and if it is also the case that our destiny is a "new heavens and new earth," then it follows they are the same – the latter expression being merely a symbol for the former. Passages which appear to suggest an earth that "abides forever" (Psa. 78:69; 104:5; Eccl. 1:4), employ the term "forever" in a *limited* sense. For instance, "forever" (Heb. *olam*) is used to modify the Jewish Passover and the Hebrew priesthood (Ex. 12:14; Num. 25:13), both of which obviously were *temporal* – lasting only so long as they were designed to remain.

HEBREWS, BOOK OF

Certain first-century Jews sought to persuade Christians (perhaps in the region of Jerusalem) to abandon the faith, return to Judaism, and wait for the *real* Messiah. The design of this letter, by an author whose identity has been concealed, is to inoculate against this danger of apostasy. The letter argues the case that Christianity is superior to Judaism, the latter being merely a divine preparation for the former. The term "better" (twelve times) is a key. The New Covenant has a better: prophet, priesthood, promises, hope, etc. A return to Judaism will signal disaster for those who succumb to the temptation.

HELL

Three different Greek words are rendered "hell" in the King James translation of the Bible. (a) *Hades* is found ten times in the Greek N.T.; nine times it is rendered "hell," once "grave" in the KJV. "Hell" is not a good rendition; it leaves a woefully faulty impression. Hades is the place of departed spirits for that period of time between death and the resurrection. See-HADES. (b) Once *tartarus* is translated as "hell" (2 Pet. 2:4). In this text the term denotes the place of punishment for rebellious angels, and may be the designation for the place in Hades where the wicked reside in general – until the day of judgment. (c) The most common word for "hell" is *gehenna* (twelve times in the N.T., eleven of these in the Synoptics). The word is a transliteration of an O.T. term meaning "valley of Hinnom" (2 Kgs. 23:10). This was the place, in the dark days of Israel, where children were sacrificed to the god Molech, hence, it was a region of *suffering* and *weeping* (2 Kg. 16:3; 21:6; Jer. 7:32; 19:6). Later, it also became the city dump, where the *burning was continuous.* The word was adopted as a symbol for the eternal, conscious punishment of the wicked, both in body and soul (Mt. 10:28), following the judgment.

HERESY, SECT

"Heresy" takes its rise from the Greek, *hairesis* (nine times in the N.T.). Originally, the term meant simply "to choose" (Lev. 22:18, 21 – LXX). Then it came to signify a choice, i.e., an opinion – especially a destructive opinion in the N.T. (2 Pet. 2:1). The term also takes on the sense of a sect that adopts an opinion contrary to divine revelation. Both the Pharisees and the Sadducees were "sects" that distorted the law of Moses (Acts 5:17, 15:5). The early Christians were charged with being a "sect" (Acts 24:14; 28:22) as they were erroneously perceived to be but an off-shoot of Judaism. The expression also can be used for a factious element (that follows an opinion, or dominate leader) within the church (1 Cor. 11:19; Gal. 5:20).

HOLY

"Holy" is from the Greek *hagios*, which carries the idea of something "separated" from other things. (a) God utterly stands apart from sinful man, and thus he is absolutely holy (Isa. 6:3; Rev. 4:8), as is Christ (Heb. 7:26), and the *Holy* Spirit. (b) Certain objects may be deemed "holy" by virtue of their use in the divine scheme of things, e.g., the "holy place" within the tabernacle (Ex. 26:33). (c) Christians are considered to be "holy" (1 Pet. 1:15; 2:9) because they have been set apart from the world by their obedience to the gospel (Eph. 5:26 – "sanctified" is the verbal form, *hagiazo*). "Saints" (*hagios*) are holy only in a *relative* sense. See SAINTS, SANCTIFIED.

HOLY SPIRIT

The Holy Spirit is a divine being who is "spirit" in nature (Lk. 24:39), and "holy" in character. (a) The Holy Spirit is not a *mere force* (as some cultists insist, e.g., the "Jehovah's Witnesses"); rather, he is an individual entity, a person, who speaks, teaches, helps, etc. (1 Tim. 4:1; Jn. 14:26; Rom. 8:26). (b) The Spirit is a separate person from both the Father and the Son (Mt. 28:19; Jn. 14:16; 15:26). (c) He possesses the very nature of God (Acts 5:3-4). (d) He empowered Christ (Jn. 3:34-35; Acts 10:38), the apostles (Acts 1:5; 2:4), and certain persons upon whom the apostles laid their hands (Acts 8:18; 19:6) to perform supernatural works as a validation of their messages. (e) The Spirit endowed the household of Cornelius with the ability to speak supernaturally in other languages in order to establish the fact that Gentiles were to be granted the gospel (Acts 10, 11). (f) Christians receive the Holy Spirit (in a nonmiraculous measure) when they are baptized into Christ (Acts 2:38; 1 Cor. 6:19; Gal. 4:6). The Spirit assists God's children in their prayers (Rom. 8:26). (g) The Spirit directed the writers of the Bible in the messages which they produced (2 Sam. 23:2; Acts 1:16; 1 Tim. 4:1) so that these documents can be accepted as the very words of God (1 Thes. 2:13).

HOMOSEXUAL

Homosexual activity is sexual intimacy between two persons of the same gender. This form of sexual conduct is uniformly condemned in the Bible. (a) It stands outside the divinely prescribed realm of authorized sexual gratification, i.e., the marriage union (Gen. 2:24; Mt. 19:4; 1 Cor. 7:2), and is, therefore, transgression (1 Jn. 3:4). (b) It is mentioned first within the community of ancient Sodom, where it receives the judgment of God (Gen. 18:20ff; 2 Pet. 2:6-8). (c) Moses' law strictly condemned homosexual conduct and made it a capital crime (Lev. 20:13). (d) Jesus upbraided homosexuality when he endorsed the original marriage law of God (Mt. 19:4), and denounced fornication explicitly (Mt. 15:19; Mk. 7:21) – which embraces homosexuality (Jude 7; cf. Mt. 11:23-24; Lk. 17:29). See: FORNICATION. (e) The apostles of Christ rebuked this immoral conduct (Rom. 1:26-27; 1 Cor. 6:9; 1 Tim. 1:9; 2 Pet. 2:6), and they wrote with divine authority (Lk. 10:16; 1 Cor. 14:37).

HOSEA, BOOK OF

Hosea lived in that era just prior to the Assyrian invasion of the kingdom of Israel (722/21 B.C.). His mission was to admonish Israel for her idolatry (Baal worship), and to urge her to repentance. The prophet's own adulterous wife is used as an illustration of the unfaithfulness of the people, Jehovah's abiding love for them, and his longing for their return to faithfulness.

HUMANITY (OF CHRIST)

The Scriptures emphatically teach that the Second Person of the Godhead, the Word (Jn. 1:1), actually became a flesh and blood human being (Jn. 1:14; Heb. 2:14). One partakes of the spirit of antichrist who denies such (2 Jn. 7). See ANTI-CHRIST. The humanity of Jesus was essential in order that he might die (Heb. 2:14), for without that death no remission of sins could be enjoyed (Heb. 9:14; 22; 10:4; 1 Pet. 1:19). The Lord's humanity is seen in his hunger (Mt. 4:2), his weariness (Jn. 4:6), his fear (Heb. 5:7), etc. Christ's humanness also qualified him to be the perfect mediator on behalf of his people (1 Tim. 2:5; Heb. 2:17-18).

IDOLATRY

Idolatry is the worship of any being or object other than the true God, and the worship of supposed images of Jehovah himself (Ex. 20:3-6). A more subtle form of idolatry is the slavish yielding to one's passions (Phil. 3:19; Col. 3:5). Idolatry is strongly condemned and, if persisted in, will lead to eternal ruin (1 Cor. 6:9; Gal. 5:20-21). See GODS.

IMMORTALITY

Two Greek words express the idea of immortality – *athanasia* (no death), and *aphtharsia* (no corruption). In the absolute sense, only God possesses immortality, i.e., an underived and unending existence (1 Tim. 6:16). Concerning those who are created in God's image (human beings exclusively), we possess an *inward spirit* that will never be subject to extinction, thus, in that sense, is *immortal* (cf. Gen. 1:26; 9:6; Heb. 12:9; 1 Pet. 3:4). Materialists, who believe that wicked men will be annihilated ultimately, deny this. See ANNIHILATION. Death does not destroy the human soul (Eccl. 12:7; Mt. 10:28; Rev. 6:9-11). At the time of the resurrection, man's body will also assume an immortal form and abide forever – whatever the nature of its destiny (Mt. 10:28; 1 Cor. 15:45-48; 2 Cor. 5:1ff; Phil. 3:21). The concept of immortality was not defined as clearly in the O.T. as it is in the New – by virtue of Christ's resurrection from the dead (2 Tim. 1:10; Rev. 1:18).

INCORPORATION, CHURCH

As noted earlier (see: CHURCH), the "church" is a body of baptized believers, called by the gospel from the "world" into a special fellowship with Christ. One must acknowledge, however, that the church exists in the modern world of law and business. Christians are permitted to use the protection of civil government when there is no breach of fidelity to Christ, and when such is expedient (see Acts 25:11; Rom. 13:1ff). One legal device at the church's disposal is the practice of "incorporation." A corporation is a "legal entity" which exists only in contemplation of law. It is a lawful mechanism which creates a protective barrier between the "corporation" as such, and the individual members who compose the organism. Churches incorporate for certain legal benefits (e.g., a tax-exempt status), and for protection (e.g., against frivolous lawsuits). It is important to note that "incorporating" does not change the basic nature or status of the organism and/or person being incorporated. A church, incorporated or otherwise, is still just a church. This procedure does not violate any scriptural principle, and is a judicious method of conducting church business in a complex legal world.

INFALLIBLE

This term means "without error." In theology, it denotes the position that the Scriptures, in their original form (the autographs), were without error. Moreover, the divine documents were inerrant in *all* areas of knowledge – history, science, moral teaching, and religious instruction (cf. Psa. 119:160 ASV). While there certainly are differences in parallel narratives (which show lack of collusion on the part of the writers), there are no *bona fide* contradictions. See: CONTRADICTION. In Roman Catholic dogma, there is the assertion of "Papal Infallibility." This is the idea that when the Pope speaks *ex cathedra* ("from the chair") on matters of morals and doctrine, he speaks without error. This teaching was promulgated initially at the First Vatican Council in 1870, and is without any semblance of Bible sanction.

INHERIT, INHERITANCE

The Greek term, found in various forms about forty-five times in the N.T., means "the possession of a lot," or portion. Some ideas associated with the word are these: (a) It can suggest a possession by right of *birth* (Gal. 4:30; Heb. 1:4; cf. Jn. 3:3-5; Gal. 3:26-27, 29). (b) The inheritance is *bestowed graciously, not earned* (Rom. 6:23). (c) There can be *conditions* associated with the reception of an inheritance (Rev. 21:7). (d) It can be *cancelled* due to lack of fidelity (Num. 14:12). (e) Its ultimate realization is in *heaven* (1 Pet. 1:4), not on earth (Mt. 6:19).

INFANTS

Contrary to the denominational claim that infants are born in sin, the Bible teaches otherwise. (a) Children do not inherit evil from their parents (Ezek. 18:20). (b) The practice of sin begins in "youth" (Gen. 9:21), not at birth. (c) Both Jesus and Paul used little children as models to be emulated in some respects (Mt. 18:3-4; 19:14; 1 Cor. 14:20). This admonition hardly would have been appropriate if infants were little "totally depraved" sinners. (d) Man "goes" astray; he is not born astray (Isa. 53:6). (e) Humans become sinners by means of their *own* sins (see Eph. 2:1 "your" – ASV), not by means of another's transgression. (f) Sin is a matter of choice, not chance (Josh. 24:15; Isa. 7:15). See: BORN IN SIN. No one ever suggested that infants are sinners until the mid-to-late second century A.D.

INSPIRATION

In his second letter to Timothy, Paul stated that the Scriptures are "inspired of God" (2 Tim. 3:16-17). The Greek is one word, *theopneustos*, literally "God breathed." It is an affirmation that God is the ultimate author of the Bible. Inspiration cannot be explained precisely in a manner that human understanding can fathom completely. In some fashion, God was able to use certain men, preserving their personal literary abilities and traits, yet overseeing the process so that the exact will of the divine mind was conveyed through the human instrument (1 Cor. 2: 11ff). The Bible contains a wide variety of evidences that establish its heavenly origin. Its inspiration is demonstrated by: (a) An amazing *unity* – some forty people produced sixty-six documents over a span of sixteen centuries. (b) Phenomenal *prophecy* – more than 1,000. Amazingly, history written in advance (see Isa. 53, for example). (c) Uncanny *accuracy*, defying human explanation. See, for instance, the numerous details in the book of Acts. (d) The Bible also evidences divine control in authorship by virtue of what it does *not* say. It contains no description of God or Christ. It omits most of Jesus' thirty-three years upon the earth, etc. These are matters that surely would have been included in a work of human design.

(e) The early writers, e.g., Paul and Peter, were willing to die rather than forfeit their claim that they were spokesmen for God in the documents they produced. See: BIBLE.

INTERCESSION

The idea of "intercession" is expressed in both Testaments of the Bible. The Greek verb *entunchano* suggests the concept of making an appeal to someone with reference to another person. It can mean to make an appeal *against* another, as when the Jews "made suit" to Festus that Paul should not live (Acts 25: 24). Normally, though, an intercession is an appeal *on behalf of* others. In such cases, it reflects a deep love for, and interest in, the one for whom the intercession is made. (a) Abraham pled for the preservation of ancient Sodom (Gen. 18:23ff). Both Moses and Elijah interceded on behalf of Israel (Ex. 32: 31-32; 1 Kgs. 18:36-37). (b) Jesus pled to God in the interest of the disciples in those dark hours before the crucifixion (Jn. 17:5), and, as our high priest, he intercedes for his people yet (Rom. 8:34; Heb. 7:25; cf. 9:24). (c) The Holy Spirit intercedes for Christians inasmuch as the children of God, sincere though they may be, do not know how to pray adequately (Rom. 8: 26). (d) Christians are to offer intercessory prayers to God on behalf of civil rulers, to the end that tranquil conditions might prevail. The goal of these prayers is that a peaceful environment might facilitate the work of evangelism, because God would have all men exposed to the truth so that they might enjoy salvation (1 Tim. 2:1-4).

ISAIAH, BOOK OF

Isaiah was a prophet who lived in Judah in the eighth century before Christ. He foretold coming judgments from God to be visited upon Israel, Judah, and several heathen nations, because of their sins. Out of that dark background, however, he also predicted a future "comfort" (18 times) from the Lord. Isaiah is called the Messianic prophet because of his emphasis upon the coming Savior (cf. chapter 53).

ISRAEL

After Jacob had his famous encounter with the "messenger" of Jehovah (Gen. 32:29; cf. Hos. 12:4-5), his name was changed to "Israel," suggesting, "he who strove with God." Later, the name is applied to the descendants of Jacob generally (Gen. 32:32; Ex. 1:9; 12:3). When the kingdom split during the days of Rehoboam, the ten tribes of the northern kingdom became known as "Israel," being distinguished from "Judah" in the south – though occasionally the southern kingdom is referred to as "Israel" as well (Isa. 8:14). When the Mosaic law was abrogated (Rom. 7:1ff; Eph. 2:11ff; Col. 2:14ff), old Israel was taken away – the final demise coming with the Roman assault in A.D. 70. The new "Israel" is the kingdom of Christ (Rom. 2:28-29; Gal. 3:26-27, 29; 6:16; Mt. 21:43; 1 Pet. 2:9). There is no promise of the "restoration" of Israel, as alleged by dispensationalists and premillennialists. Old Testament promises of restoration pertained either to: (a) a restoration of the exiles from the Babylonian captivity; or, (b) the *spiritual* restoration to be effected in the church (Acts 3:21-24). Note the connection in this latter passage between "restoration" and "these days," i.e., the days of the Christian age (vv. 21, 24).

JAMES, BOOK OF

This book, authored by the Lord's half-brother (Gal. 1:19), is directed to the "twelve tribes scattered abroad." This is either Jewish Christians, or a figurative designation for "spiritual Israel" (Gal. 6:16), the church generally. The narrative is sometimes characterized as the "gospel of practical Christianity." It has two major thrusts. First, it is aimed at encouraging the saints in times of persecution (1:2-4). Too, the book admonishes that valid faith is that which acts in obeying God; faith without obedience is dead (2:14ff). This letter is a problem for those who allege that salvation is by "faith alone" (cf. 2:24).

JEHOVAH

"Jehovah" is a name for God that is found in the American Standard Version (1901) of the O.T. The word is actually a hybrid term, composed of four Hebrew consonants, YHWH, and vowel sounds taken from the name "Lord" (*Adonai*). The term "Jehovah" attempts to approximate the original term, but *Yahweh* is probably a closer guess, the original having been lost due to the Jewish superstition of not wanting to actually pronounce the sacred name. YHWH is found more than 6,800 times in the O.T. (LORD – all caps in most translations); it is the special name which the Lord gave to distinguish himself from the gods of the heathen world (Ex. 3:13-15). It expressed a special covenant relationship between God and Israel. The name generally is believed to be associated with a verb that means "to be," thus suggesting the idea of a *self-existing* being, one with unoriginated existence (cf. Ex. 3:14). The fact that Jesus identified himself with this expression (Jn. 8:58), and that the prophets heralded the coming of "Jehovah" (Isa. 40:3), is clear testimony to the deity of Christ.

JEREMIAH, BOOK OF

The southern kingdom of Judah had sunk deep into apostasy. The prophet Jeremiah was raised up to offer them God's final invitation for repentance. When that failed, the prophet was commissioned to foretell the coming Babylonian conquest, and to admonish the nation that it must submit to the punishing invasion and subsequent captivity – for seventy years. The prophet was sorely persecuted for his courageous message. Jeremiah also denounced the sins of several pagan nations.

JESUS CHRIST

The names "Jesus Christ" mean "savior" and "anointed," suggesting that this noble person was "anointed" of God (Acts 10:38) to be prophet, priest, and king, and indeed, the Savior of the world (Mt. 1:21). The following facts about Jesus are paramount: (a) He existed eternally as the divine Word, before his incarnation (Mic. 5:2; Jn. 1:1ff; 8:58). In the O.T. era, he operated on behalf of the Lord's people as the ANGEL or MESSENGER OF JEHOVAH (see this reference) in a preliminary capacity before entering the world as a human being. (b) He was conceived miraculously by the power of the Holy Spirit, and born to Mary, a virgin (Lk. 1:35; Isa. 7:14; Mt. 1:22-23). He thus is the Son of God, being both divine and human in nature (Jn. 1:14). (c) He performed numerous miracles that validated his claim of having come from heaven (Jn. 6:48-50; 20:30-31). (d) He committed no sin (Heb. 4:15; 1 Pet. 2:22) and therefore was qualified to die as an atonement for the sins of humanity (Rom. 3:21ff; 2 Cor. 5:21). (e) He was raised from the dead, which act declared him to be the Son of God with power (Rom. 1:4). (f) He ascended back to his Father where he presently reigns as king (Acts 2:29ff). (g) At an appointed time,

Christ will return to claim his own and render judgment upon all (Acts 17:31; 1 Thes. 4:13ff). (h) Jesus is the exclusive means of salvation (Jn. 14:6; Acts 4:11-12), the only hope of mankind for heaven (Col. 1:27). The historical evidence for Jesus' existence is overwhelming. It is established by the N.T. documents – all of which date within the first century. Jewish writings also contain references to Christ (e.g., the Talmud and Josephus). Even pagan writings (e.g., Tacitus and Seutonius) mention him. The testimony of early Christian documents concerning Christ (e.g., Polycarp, Ignatius, etc.) are profuse. There is no reasonable explanation for Jesus and his amazing influence, save for the fact that he lived, and was actually who he claimed to be, the Christ – Son of God (Mk. 14:62).

JOB, BOOK OF

This celebrated book is a narrative regarding an ancient patriarch who lived in Arabia. As a test case, designed to prove that God is "worthy to be praised" (Psa. 18:3) irrespective of the blessings he bestows, Job becomes a tragic, yet faithful example, of endurance (Jas. 5:11). He lost his wealth, his children, his health, and his friends, yet he clung to his confidence that God would vindicate him eventually (19:25-27), in spite of his confused and weak moments. The book demonstrates that even the best of the Lord's people are not exempt from suffering, and that our Maker must be trusted – no matter what happens (13:15).

JOEL, BOOK OF

Joel, a prophet of the southern kingdom of Judah, labors to warn the Hebrew people of the coming "day of the Lord," a time of judgment upon a rebellious people. The punishment is described under a dreaded plague of locust. Those who remain faithful, however, will be blessed. Joel predicts the outpouring of the Holy Spirit on the day of Pentecost (2:28ff).

JOHN, BOOK OF

The first three Gospel accounts (Matthew, Mark, and Luke) are called SYNOPTICS (see), because they view the life of Christ from roughly the same vantagepoint. John's account is different. His record is not addressed to a particular segment of society; rather, it is cosmopolitan in nature. John's Gospel starts at the very "beginning" of time, emphasizing that the Word (Christ) was in existence eternally (1:1, 14). The Fourth Gospel is very selective, focusing upon slightly more than thirty days of Jesus' ministry (which lasted three and one-half years). It especially stresses the "signs" performed by the Lord, noting that these establish the fact that he is "the Christ, the Son of God" (20:30-31).

JOHN FIRST, BOOK OF

John's first epistle is a defense against the "gnostic" doctrine that alleged that Jesus Christ was not a real, flesh-and-blood human being. This sect claimed a special "knowledge" received directly from God. Contrary to this false claim, it is the Christian who can "know" (some thirty-five times, represented by two Greek words) the truth regarding the Lord. The apostle encourages the brethren to refrain from sin (2:1), so that their joy might be made full (1:4). There is much encouragement to love the brethren in this book.

A Practical Handbook

JOHN SECOND, BOOK OF

John's second epistle is a word of commendation for a certain "elect lady" and her children. Further, it provides strong warnings regarding those who go beyond the teaching of Christ, and cautions against giving endorsement (via hospitality) to those who undermine the doctrine of the Lord.

JOHN THIRD, BOOK OF

This book is an appeal to a godly Christian whose name was Gaius, to the end that this brother might assist certain workers who were laboring on behalf of the Lord. Additionally, it conveys a strong warning concerning a "church bully" named Diotrephes who sought to glorify himself. John promises he will deal with this rebel if he is able to join Gaius. The epistle commends one Demetrius as well.

JONAH, BOOK OF

Nineveh was the capital city of Assyria. It was an exceedingly wicked city, but Jehovah loved even these alien Gentiles. Accordingly, he sent Jonah, a prophet from northern Palestine, to proclaim unto the citizens a message of repentance. Jonah rebelled at this mission, heading west instead of east. God caused him to be thrown into the sea where he was swallowed by a huge fish. After three days of "education" in a sub-marine classroom, Jonah decided to do as the Lord had commanded. He went to Nineveh and proclaimed God's message. The people of Nineveh repented and were spared (for another century and a half). The confinement of Jonah in the fish's belly was a pictorial preview of Jesus' stay in the tomb (Mt. 12:40-41).

JOSEPHUS, FLAVIUS

A Jewish historian who lived around A.D. 37-103. He was initially a resister against the Roman invasion of Judaea (A.D. 70), but he surrendered eventually. He went to Rome where he was commissioned to write a history of the Jewish people. He mentions both John the Baptist and Jesus. Of Christ he wrote: "Now there was about this time Jesus, a wise man, if it be lawful to call him a man; for he was a doer of wonderful works, a teacher of such men as receive the truth with pleasure. He drew over to him both many of the Jews and many of the Gentiles. He was Christ. And when Pilate, at the suggestion of the principal men among us, had condemned him to the cross, those that loved him at the first did not forsake him; for he appeared to them alive again the third day; as the divine prophets had foretold these and ten thousand other wonderful things concerning him. And the tribe of Christians, so named from him, are not extinct at this day" (*Antiquities* 18.3.3.). While many writers dispute portions of this statement, it has been defended quite ably – in its entirety – by very competent scholars.

JOSHUA, BOOK OF

This book contains the record of Israel's conquest of the land of Canaan. The leader of the campaign was Joshua, who substantially took the land in three military invasions – first, the central region, then the south, and finally the north. The document thus pictures the fulfillment of the land promise that Jehovah had made to Abraham, Isaac, and Jacob. The book covers about thirty years of Israel's history – from the death of Moses to the death of Joshua.

JUDE, BOOK OF

Jude, a brother of James, and half-brother of Jesus (1:1; Mt. 13:55), is the author of this general epistle. As he was in the process of beginning a letter relative to the "common salvation," he was constrained to pen a warning concerning certain false teachers who, under cover, were attacking the nature and work of Christ. At the same time, they were changing the gospel of grace into a message that allowed lascivious conduct. Jude apparently follows up on Peter's similar warnings (cf. 2 Pet. 2:3 – 3:4). The book provides both caution and encouragement to Christians.

JUDGE, JUDGING

The Greek word *krino* means to render a verdict (Lk. 7:43; Acts 15:9). Prepositions may be attached as prefixes to provide some direction to the term. For example, *diakrino* suggests the idea of distinguishing between objects (1 Cor. 6:5; 11:31; 14:19); *anakrino* means to investigate or thoroughly scrutinize (1 Cor. 2:14; 4:3). Jesus once said: "Judge not..." (a prohibition), and then again, he said: "Judge ye..." (an imperative). Obviously, there is a *wrong* way to judge and a *right* way. (a) One must not judge superficially, i.e., according to appearance (Jn. 7:24a). Judgment should not be done hypocritically (Mt. 7:3-5; Rom. 2:1ff). (b) Yet one must judge himself (1 Cor. 11:31; cf. 2 Cor. 13:5). Sometimes one must judge others, i.e., pronounce judgment concerning them (1 Cor. 5:3; 6:2-4). But always, he is to judge "righteous" judgment (Jn. 7:24b), i.e., a judgment measured by divine truth. (c) God, as a perfect being, has every right to judge according to righteousness (Gen. 18:25; Ezek. 33:20; 2 Tim. 4:1; Rev. 19:2). (d) Final judgment will be effected through Christ (Acts 17:31; 2 Cor. 5:10).

JUDGES, BOOK OF

The book of Judges narrates the administrations of fifteen national leaders (judges, deliverers) during that era when the land of Canaan was being settled by the Hebrew people. It covers a period of more than three hundred years – from the death of Joshua to that of Samson. The book reveals the cycles of apostasy, punishment, and deliverance through which the nation passed during this troubling time in its history.

JUDGMENT DAY

This is a specific time determined by God for the vindication of divine operation. Acts 17:31 is a very comprehensive passage in this regard: (a) A day of judgment has been "appointed." (b) The entire "world" will be judged (cf. Gen. 18:25; Mt. 25:32; Rev. 20:11-12). (c) Judgment will be according to a standard of "righteousness," i.e., the law of God under which one has lived (cf. Rom. 2:16; Rev. 20:12); those standards will be compared with the deeds of one's life (2 Cor. 5:10). (d) Judgment will be effected by Christ, who is completely qualified to assume that role, with no quibbling by humanity. (e) Judgment will be proportional, i.e., equitable (Mt. 11:20ff; Heb. 10:28-29; Jas. 3:1). (f) The day of judgment will not be to *determine* one's fate. One's destiny is known at the point of death (Lk. 16:23ff; 2 Pet. 2:9 ASV); rather, it will be the time of the "revelation of the righteous judgment of God" (Rom. 2:5). At this point, there will be no atheists, no critics of God, for every knee shall bow and every tongue will confess (Rom. 14:11-12). The notion that the judgment day has already passed, having occurred in A.D. 70, as taught by some, is a false idea (see REALIZED ESCHATOLOGY).

JUSTICE

Justice may be viewed from two vantage points. *Divine* justice, i.e., that which is between God and man; and, *human* justice, that which exists between men. (a) Divine justice has to do with the harmony between the absolutely holy nature of God, and his dealings with sinful creatures. God is a being of utter holiness (Isa. 6:3; Rev. 4:8), and holiness demands the punishment of sin (Hab. 1:13); sin is so contrary to God's nature (Jas. 1:13). Sin cannot be ignored. Justice demands a penalty (Rom. 6:23), and God is just (Gen. 18:25; Psa. 89:14; 119:137-138). However, the Lord is also loving and merciful (1 Jn. 4:8; Eph. 2:4). Is there a solution by which God's love and his justice may be reconciled? Indeed! And that was by means of the death of his Son, i.e., the death of an *innocent* victim, Christ (Isa. 53:11; Rom. 3:26). Here, then, is the case. Either man, by surrendering to the will of Christ, will allow the Savior to assume the punishment for him, or he will endure it for himself in hell. In any event, God's justice will be satisfied. (b) Human justice has to do with the fact that men must live together in an orderly society. Law exists for the lawless (1 Tim. 1:8-9). Men who do not live by the rule of law must be punished, and civil government is the instrument of God to this end (Rom. 13:1ff; 1 Pet. 2:13-17). Rulers who take bribes, or in other ways thwart justice, will be held accountable by the King of kings and Lord of lords (Rev. 19:11-16).

JUSTIFICATION

Justification may be defined as the divine process by which God acquits the sinner and reckons him as righteous. The noun *dikaiosis* ("justification") is used but twice in the N.T. (Rom. 4:25; 5:18). The verb *dikaioo* is employed thirty-nine times in the N.T., and it describes the *result* of the process of justification. There are some exceedingly erroneous ideas regarding justification in the religious community. The Roman Catholic dogma of justification on the basis of meritorious works does not conform to the teaching of the N.T. (Eph. 2:8-9; Tit. 3:5). The reactionary doctrine of Protestantism that justification is on the ground of "faith alone" is equally spurious (Gal. 5:6; Jas. 2:14ff; esp. 24). Biblical justification involves: (a) All accountable people are sinners (Rom. 3:10, 23), and therefore deserving of condemnation (Rom. 6:23); if there is to be any hope for fallen humanity, a process of justification must be divinely *extended.* (b) No person can *earn* justification (Mt. 18:21ff), or *merit* it (Eph. 2:8-9). (c) Justification can be extended only on the basis of Christ's death as the sinless sacrifice for man (1 Pet. 1:19; Rom. 3:24-26). (d) Justification will be bestowed only when man responds to God's plan by faith (Rom. 3:26; 5:1). It is the *nature* of that "faith" that is crucial to this issue. In the book of Romans, as elsewhere in the N.T., faith is not mere mental assent, or even a disposition simply to trust the Lord. Rather, it is a willingness to *submit* to the requirements mandated by the Creator. Faith issues in *obedience* (Rom. 1: 5; 16:26). Note this: Man is justified by faith (Rom. 5:1). But "justification" is the equivalent of being "free from sin," (Rom. 6:18), which results from one having been "obedient from the heart" to the "pattern" of gospel teaching (Rom. 6:17). Thus, justification is predicated upon obedience (cf. Heb. 5:8-9). "Justification," or "being made free from sin," occurs when one is "raised" to walk in "newness of life" (Rom. 6:4b). The process of justification is therefore consummated when one is "buried with [Christ] through baptism" (6:4a). (e) Finally, the *result* of justification is "peace with God" and a rejoicing in "hope of the glory of God" (Rom. 5:1-2).

KINDNESS

Kindness (*chrestos*) may be defined as that which is characterized by honesty, friendliness, goodness, generosity, compassion, etc. The term is used in the N.T. in two main senses. (a) Kindness describes the attitude and actions of God toward the rebellious human race. Heaven's kindness is not fickle, as is the case with flawed humanity; it endures forever (Psa. 106:1). It was manifest in the plan of redemption (Eph. 2:7ff; Tit. 3:4), and is the motivation for our obedience (see: Lk. 6:35; Rom. 2:4 – *chreston* "goodness"). (b) Kindness is a most desirable trait in people (Prov. 19:22). It is a quality in those who possess love for others (1 Cor. 13:4; cf. Prov. 31:26). Kindness is a fruit of the indwelling presence of the Holy Spirit (Gal. 5:22), and it is the cement that holds brothers in Christ together (Eph. 4:31-32).

KING

This is the title of a sovereign who exercises regal authority over a certain territory. The term is used in the following senses in Scripture. (a) Jehovah God is king over the entire earth (1 Sam. 12:12; Mt. 22:7; 1 Tim. 6:16). (b) The title is sometimes used of the political rule of certain earthly dignitaries (Mt. 2:1; 1 Pet. 2:13). (c) It is employed as well of the role of Christ. Christ's reign was prophesied in the O.T. (Psa. 110; 2 Sam. 7:12-13; Zech. 6:12-13). It commenced when he ascended to the Father following his resurrection (Acts 2:30ff; Eph. 1:20ff; Heb. 1:3; 1 Pet. 3:22; cf. Mk. 9:1; Acts 1:8; 2:4). Christ's reign will continue (in his *mediatorial* capacity) until the time of his return for judgment (1 Cor. 15:24-25). There is a sense, of course, in which Jesus will reign for ever (Rev. 3:21; 5:13). That Christ will *not* return to reign *upon the earth* (as millennialism alleges) is evidenced by the fact that he is to be *both* king and priest *simultaneously* (Psa. 110; Zech. 6:12-13), and yet he cannot serve as priest *on earth* (Heb. 8:4; 7:14). It must be noted in conclusion that Christ has authority "over all flesh," (Jn. 17:3), i.e., universally (Mt. 28:18; cf. Rev. 1:5), though some reject him as sovereign (Lk. 19:14), and will suffer the consequences for that action (Lk. 19:27).

KINGDOM

The word "kingdom" (*basileia*) is a noun that generally refers to a territory over which a king rules. Three senses are prominent in the theology of the N.T. (a) Jesus uses the term to denote the reign of God over the *nation of Israel* (Mt. 21:43). That divine system would become obsolete with the termination of the Mosaic system, being replaced by a new kingdom, the church (1 Pet. 2:9-10). The destruction of Judaism in A.D. 70 was Jehovah's epitaph upon the Hebrews as a favored nation. (b) The term "kingdom" is commonly used in the N.T. as an equivalent to the "church," the former expression emphasizing the administrative composition of the Lord's regime, the latter stressing its relationship to the world. The terms "church" and "kingdom" are used interchangeably at times (cf. Mt. 16:18-19; Lk. 22:29-30 with 1 Cor. 10:16; Jn. 3:3-5 with 1 Cor. 12:13; Col. 1:18; Heb. 12:23, 28). The kingdom is entered when the believing penitent is baptized in water (Jn. 3:3-5; 1 Cor. 12:13; Gal. 3:27). Acceptable worship is rendered *within* that domain (Lk. 22:29-30). (c) The word "kingdom" also may refer to the final, *heavenly* state of blessedness in which the people of God will abide eternally (2 Tim. 4:13; 2 Pet. 1:11), i.e., heaven itself. The theory (called premillennialism) that Jesus intended to set up his kingdom at the time of his *first* coming, but postponed that enterprise due to a surprising rejection by the Jews, and so, will establish the kingdom at the time of his *second* coming, is false. See DISPENSATIONALISM.

KINGS 1, BOOK OF

This historical book covers a period of about 126 years – from the death of David, Israel's great king, to the death of Jehoshaphat, one of Judah's rulers. It embraces the reign of Solomon, the tragic division of the people in the reign of Jeroboam (who led Israel into idolatry), and the conflicts between the weak king, Ahab, and the courageous prophet, Elijah.

KINGS 2, BOOK OF

This document is a historical narrative of a period of about 270 years, from the time of Jehoshaphat's death, to the fall of Jerusalem, when Judah's final group was taken into Babylonian captivity – and even slightly beyond (2 Kgs. 25:27). The book tells of the closing days of Elijah the prophet, and his successor, Elisha. It chronicles the Assyrian conquest of Israel, and the overall history of the nation between the Assyrian invasion (722/21 B.C.) and the fall of Jerusalem (586 B.C.).

KNOWLEDGE

Knowledge refers to a body of factual data that is received and understood by a rational human being. The acquisition of *spiritual* knowledge is fundamental to Christianity. The prophets foretold that those of the Christian era who faithfully serve God will be those who "know" him (Jer. 31:31-34). Jesus declared: "It is written in the prophets, And they shall all be *taught* of God. Every one that has heard from the Father, and has *learned*, comes unto me" (Jn. 6:45). Knowing the "truth" is prerequisite to being set free from sin (Jn. 8:32), and the knowledge of that truth is in the word of God (Jn. 17:17; 1 Tim. 2:4). While there is a rudimentary level of "knowledge" which testifies that there is such a thing as "right" and "wrong" (Rom. 2:14-15), the full body of spiritual knowledge necessary to please God is not intuitive. Nor is divine knowledge accessed directly by some sort of "personal encounter" with deity, or by a supernatural outpouring of the Holy Spirit. Rather, sacred knowledge has been deposited in that body of literature known as the Scriptures (2 Tim. 3:16-17). Paul reminded the Ephesian saints that the revelation of God's will had been made known unto him by "words," which, he said, "when you read" you can "perceive my understanding" (Eph. 3:1ff). To those pseudo-sophisticated moderns, who believe that spiritual knowledge and truth are unattainable, Scripture replies: "We *know* that the Son of God is come and hath given us an *understanding*, that we might *know* him that is *truth"* (1 Jn. 5:20). The term "know" is also used in the New Testament in the sense of "obey." "And hereby we know that we know him, if we keep his commandments" (1 Jn. 2:3).

LAMB OF GOD

The imagery of a "lamb" is taken from the O.T. to convey certain thoughts about Christ. John the Baptizer introduced Jesus as the "lamb of God who takes away the sin of the world" (Jn. 1:29). The Passover lamb of the O.T. was clearly a "type" (see) of Christ (1 Cor. 5:7). There are several important truths associated with this idea. (a) Christ was a *spotless* lamb with no blemish (cf. Ex. 12:5; 1 Pet. 1:19). It was this sinless character that allowed him to die as a sacrifice for sin (2 Cor. 5:21). (b) Christ was *submissive* to the will of God. "He was oppressed, yet when he was afflicted he opened not his mouth; as a lamb that is led to the slaughter, and as a sheep that before its shearers is dumb, so he opened not his mouth" (Isa. 53:7). His faithful obedience is an abiding example for us (1 Pet. 2:21ff). (c) Jesus was a *sacrificed* lamb (1 Cor. 5:7). His voluntary offering of himself (Gal. 1:4) was the necessary price for man's redemption (Mt. 20:28; 26:28; 1 Cor. 15:1-4). (d) Christ is portrayed as a *victorious* lamb in the book of Revelation (twenty-eight times) – a lamb that was slain (5:6, 9, 12; 13:8), but that stood up again (5:6), and is "alive for evermore" (1:18). In this final book of the N.T., the lamb is a leader of his people (7:17; 14:1-4) who were purchased by his blood (5:9-10; 14:4).

LAMENTATIONS, BOOK OF

The book of Lamentations was written by the prophet Jeremiah. It actually is a funeral song designed to commemorate the destruction of Jerusalem by the invading Babylonians (586 B.C.). The song is a sad reminder of the sins that led to the fall of the holy city, and the seventy-year long period of captivity that followed.

LANGUAGES

Prior to the incident at Babel (Gen. 11:1ff), the people of the earth spoke one language. Because of ancient man's ambition to "make a name" for himself, and due to his resistance to dispersing and filling the earth (Gen. 1:28), God "confounded" the human tongue and men began to speak languages that were not understood by one another. There are now more than

3,000 languages world-wide. While some consider the biblical account to be nothing more than myth, the evidence indicates otherwise. According to the late Max Muller of Oxford University, language studies reveal that the tongues of man have a common origin. Modern computer comparisons appear to confirm this conclusion. Ancient historical traditions among several nations, and archaeological discovery, also have suggested that there are genuine historical roots to the "Babel" account.

LANGUAGES OF THE BIBLE

The text of the Bible consists of three languages. (a) The O.T. was composed principally in Hebrew. This Semitic tongue was well adapted to emotional, poetic, and religious expression. It was ideal for the revelation of divine religion in the early days of man's history. (b) Some portions of the O.T. are in Aramaic (Dan. 2:4-4:7; Ezra 4:8-6:18; 7:12-16; Jer. 10:11). After the time of the Babylonian captivity, Aramaic replaced Hebrew as the spoken language of the Israelite people. It continued to be the tongue of the Hebrews until their destruction in A.D. 70. (c) The N.T. was penned in *KOINE* GREEK (see), the common language of commercial and street life in the first century Roman Empire. It was used from Rome to Babylon. Paul's letter to the saints in Rome was not in Latin, but Greek. *Koine* was the finest language instrument ever for the expression of precise human thought. Surely this language was a tool employed in the providential workings of God. See: FULNESS OF TIME.

LAST DAYS

Certain religionists, especially those who subscribe to the dogma of DISPENSATIONALISM (see), maintain that the "signs" of Matthew 24:1-34 indicate that the return of Christ is very near; they constantly harp that we "are living in the last days." First, the "signs" of Matthew 24:1ff are related to the destruction of Jerusalem in A.D. 70, not the time of the Lord's *final* coming (v. 34-36). Second, the expression "last days" refers to the concluding dispensation of time, the Christian age. Note: (a) Joel foretold of the pouring out of God's Spirit in "the last days" (Joel 2:28ff). On the day of Pentecost, Peter quotes this passage and applies it to the era commencing that day (cf. Acts 2:16-17). (b) God's house, the church (1 Tim. 3:15) was to be established in the last days (Isa. 2:2-4); it was established on the day of Pentecost (Acts 2:37-42, 47). (c) Paul warned Timothy of certain sins that would be prevalent in "the last days." He then admonished: "from these also *be turning away*" (1 Tim. 3:1-5). The present participle form reveals that Timothy was in the last days *at that time*. The expression "last days" does not demand, therefore, proximity to the end of the world in an imminent sense.

LAW

Law is a mandate that is designed to regulate procedure; it proceeds from a superior, who possesses authority to rule, to a subordinate. Law is viewed from several angles in the Scriptures. (a) The material Universe was made to operate according to law. For example, the moon and stars operate in harmony with "ordinances" (Jer. 31:35). (b) Angels are subject to divine law, for some of them "sinned" (2 Pet. 2:4), and sin is a transgression of law (1 Jn. 3:4; cf. Rom. 4:15). (c) From the beginning of creation, humanity was under law; both Adam and Eve sinned, hence, transgressed law (Rom. 5:12; 1 Tim. 2:14). The law of God was seriously violated during the days of Noah (Gen. 6:5; 2 Pet. 2:5), thus, the great FLOOD (see). (d) From Mount Sinai (cir. 1500 B.C.), God gave the Israelite people a law, the law of Moses. No one, save these people, were amenable to that particular law (Dt. 5:1-5). (e) From the day of Pentecost, a new law went forth (Isa. 2:2-4); it is the law of Christ (1 Cor. 9:21; Gal. 6:2). (f) Civil law exists for the protection of society (Rom. 13:1ff; 1 Pet. 2:13-16).

LAW OF MOSES

A significant portion of the Old Testament record embodies the law of Moses. Some basic facts relative to that system must be understood. (a) It was given by God, and ordained by angels; it came through Moses as a mediator (Gal. 3:19). (b) It was given at Sinai (cir. 1500 B.C.), and was terminated at the cross (Col. 2:14). (c) The law required perfect obedience, or else it brought a curse (Dt. 27:26; Gal. 3:10). (d) It was characterized by carnal ordinances (Heb. 9:10). (e) The law was designed to prepare for the coming of Christ (Gal. 3:19; 24-25). (f) It contained prophecy that indicated it would be replaced by a new covenant (Jer. 31:31-34). (g) The law was given only to the nation of Israel (Dt. 5:1-5). (h) It had only animal blood, thus, forgiveness was on a year-by-year basis (Heb. 10:1-4; cf. Heb. 9:15). (i) Ultimately, it was weak and unprofitable in terms of effecting redemption (Heb. 7:18; Gal. 4:4). (j) While the Mosaic law is not a law for Christians, it does contain many valuable historical lessons and abiding principles (Rom. 15:4).

LAYING ON OF HANDS

The act of "laying on of hands" served several functions in the N.T. (a) Some parents brought their children that Jesus might lay his hands upon them (Mt. 19:13). This involved no magical ritual; rather, it was a symbolic act designed to invoke Jehovah's blessings upon these children. (b) Laying on of hands was sometimes employed in connection with healing miracles (Mk. 6:5; Lk. 4:40; 13:13). (c) Miraculous gifts of the Holy Spirit were conveyed by the laying on of the apostles' hands (Acts 8:18; Acts 19:6; 2 Tim. 1:6). (d) The laying on of hands was employed to set men apart for special works in the Lord's service (Acts 13:3; 1 Tim. 4:14; 5:22).

LEVITICUS, BOOK OF

The third book of the Hebrew Pentateuch is Leviticus, the title of which suggests "that which pertains to the tribe of Levi." This Mosaic document provides information regarding the sacrifices, the priesthood, purifications, and festivals of the law of Moses. Many of these institutions were typical, pointing to Christ and the N.T. system. The idea of "atonement" is prominent (thirty-six times).

LIBERALISM

"Liberalism" (in the classical sense of the word) is a rather flexible term for an ideological disposition that developed in the 1800's, and reached an intense level in America during the days preceding World War II. It is characterized by several arrogant attitudes. (a) Liberalism seeks to establish a break with the rigid acknowledgement of the historical accuracy and authority of the Scriptures. Allegedly, the discoveries of the scientific community have progressively and significantly made the Bible irrelevant to the modern man. (b) Liberalism involves the exaltation of human "reason" over the testimony of scriptural history. All events in the Bible (especially the miraculous) must be measured by modern "experience," rather than judged in the light of credible, historical testimony. The supernatural events of the Scriptures are dismissed therefore. (c) Liberalism has an unbalanced view of the "benevolence" of God; all references to divine wrath, judgment, and hell are rejected, supposedly being incompatible with how God "ought" to be. (d) Since no one will finally be "lost," according to this philosophy, there is no further need for Christ (except as a vague moral example), his atoning death, resurrection, etc. These elements, therefore, are to be removed from Christianity. (e) This ideology argues for a novel view of "human freedom," i.e., man must be granted the freedom to search for himself, identify himself, and fulfill himself – without interference from a Higher Power. In brief – freedom from divine *restraint!* See EXISTENTIALISM. In reality, "liberalism" is nothing more than infidelity, merely clothed with the veneer of a quasi-religious garb.

LIFE

Life may be viewed under two categories – *physical* life and *spiritual* life. (a) All biological organisms are characterized by *physical* "life." A living creature has independent movement, processes food and oxygen, reproduces, etc. Life is a mystery that science cannot explain. It is a "gift" from God (Acts 17:25; 1 Tim. 6:13). It has been estimated that the probability of "life" starting itself is on the order of one in ten to the two-billionth power – which means it simply could not happen. Human life is sacred because man and woman exist in the image of God (Gen. 1:26; 9:6). It is therefore wrong to arbitrarily (i.e., without authority) take human life. Physical life is temporal due to the introduction of sin (Gen. 2:17; Rom. 5:12; 6:23). (b) *Spiritual* life is the state of being united with God in a Father/child relationship. The Ephesian saints, prior to their conversion to Christ, had been "dead" in their trespasses and sins, but they were "made alive" by their union with the Lord (Eph. 2:1, 5). In many passages "life" is used as the equivalent of "salvation." "For God so loved the world, that he gave his only begotten Son, that whosoever believeth on him should not perish, but have *eternal life*. For God sent not the Son into the world to judge the world; but that the world through him might be *saved*" (Jn. 3:16-17). Note the parallel expressions. Spiritual life is received when one is raised from the water of baptism (Rom. 6:4). The redeemed person's spiritual life, or communion with God, extends into heaven itself – for all who remain faithful (2 Cor. 5:4; 2 Tim. 1:10; Rev. 2:10). In the eternal order, even the wicked continue to "live" (i.e., exist), though they do not enjoy "eternal life" (Mt. 10:28; 25:46; Mk. 9:48).

LOGOS

Logos is the term used in the Gospel of John to describe the preincarnate Christ. "In the beginning was the Word [*logos*] ... and the Word [*logos*] became flesh..." (Jn. 1:1, 14). Though the term *logos* was used profusely in classical Greek in a variety of mystical ways, there is no evidence whatever that John imported the classical sense into his use of the word. Better is the idea that John's employment was grounded in a Hebraic background. In the Greek version of the O.T. (LXX), *logos* was commonly used to convey the ideas of creative power (Gen. 1:

3, 6, 9, etc.) and communicative activity (Jer. 1:4; Ezek. 1:3; Amos 3:1). In John's use of the term, with reference to Jesus, several forceful ideas are conveyed: (a) The *logos* existed eternally; the imperfect tense verbs (*en* – "was") suggests a timeless existence. (b) The *logos* was in intimate association with Jehovah ("with [*pros*] God" affirms a face-to-face closeness). (c) The *logos*, as to his essence, *is* God, i.e., deity – not "a god," as the Watchtower cult alleges. (d) The *logos* was the instrument of creative activity. (e) The *logos* "became flesh" and dwelt among men, "declaring" (providing a commentary on) the Father to them (v. 18). To know what God is like can be best discovered by studying Christ most carefully.

LORD

The Greek expression for "lord" is *kurios*. One must look at the context to observe the sense conveyed in a particular setting. "Lord" may be used as a mere title of respect, or it can suggest one who is deity. (a) *Kurios* is sometimes used in the sense of one who is owner or master of a thing, i.e., he has the authority to do as he wishes (Mt. 20:8, 15). Jesus used this term to assert his authority relative to the sabbath day (Mt. 12:8). (b) The word was sometimes employed as a mere title of respect, as in "Sir" (Jn. 4:11). In this case, while the Samaritan woman addressed Jesus as *kurios*, she had not as yet ascertained his identity. (c) *Kurios* is used of God as the ruler of the Universe (Mt. 5:33). It is used in the LXX to render several Hebrew words, e.g., *Adon, Adonai*, and *YHWH* (the sacred name of God). (d) The word was used of Christ to denote that, by his death and resurrection, he acquired authority over mankind (Acts 2:36; cf. Jn. 17:2; Eph. 1:20ff). In numerous contexts *kurios* emphasizes the deity of Jesus (Jn. 20:28; Acts 10:36;

Rom. 6:23). All genuine Christians acknowledge Jesus as the *master* of their lives, with complete authority to direct their beliefs and conduct (Mt. 28:18; Phil. 2:9-10).

LORD'S DAY

This expression is found only one time in the N.T. While on the island of Patmos, the apostle John was "in the spirit on the Lord's day" (Rev. 1:10). But the adjective, *kuriakos*, "the Lord's," is also used of the communion supper (1 Cor. 11:20). The term means "belonging to the Lord." The writers of the post-apostolic age spoke of Sunday as "the Lord's day." For example, a document, known as the *Didache*, states: "... come together each Lord's day of the Lord, break bread, and give thanks" (14). Revelation 1:10 is an obvious reference to the FIRST DAY OF THE WEEK (see).

LORD'S SUPPER

Mentioned only in 1 Corinthians 11:20. See COMMUNION.

LOST

The most common Greek word representing this idea is *apollumi*. The term can suggest the idea of an object that is estranged from its owner. A shepherd loses his sheep, a woman loses a coin, a Father loses a son (Lk. 15:4, 9, 32). When men, by their sins, wander away from their Creator, they are "lost" (Lk. 19:10; cf. Isa. 59:1-2). Only through the gospel of Christ can reconciliation be enjoyed. When *apollumi* is used in the middle voice, it denotes "irretrievable ruin" (Jn. 3:16; 17:12), though never ANNIHILILATION (see).

LOVE

The Greeks had several words that reflected various concepts of "love." Forms of three of these are found in the N.T. (a) The noun *storge* had a variety of uses in the ancient world, but it most commonly had to do with family love. Paul uses a negative form of it twice to designate those who are "without natural affection" (Rom. 1:31; 2 Tim. 3:3). This would condemn family members who abuse one another (including mothers who kill their babies), whether in the natural family or the spiritual family. In Romans 12:10 Paul joins *storgos* with *phileo* which comes out as "tenderly affectioned" in the ASV. (b) The Greek term *phileo* is a tender, affectionate love – the love of the heart. It is that which a parent would have for his child (Mt. 10:37, or the love between two close friends (Jn. 11:3, 36; 20:2). Interestingly, the word "kiss" (*philema*) is a kindred term. (c) The most predominate words for love in the N.T. are the noun *agape*, together with its corresponding verb, *agapao*. This is the love of the will. It casts aside emotions, likes and dislikes, and loves because of the worth of the object to be loved. *Agape* is the love with which God loved us, even when we were sinners, prompting him to give his own Son on our behalf (Jn. 3:16; Rom. 5:8). Nigel Turner, one of Great Britain's prominent Greek scholars, has noted that among the best of the ancient pagans (e.g., Aristotle), "God" was not expected to love human beings. Perhaps that is why *agape* was extremely rare in its usage before Christianity gave it a personality all its own. The best lexicon of *agape* is found in 1 Corinthians 13; there love is described as being patient, kind, and not envious. It is neither boastful nor proud. It behaves well, is unselfish, isn't easily irritated, and doesn't keep score on the mistakes of others. Love does not rejoice in things wrong, but is happy with truth. It is willing to overlook being wronged when possible, and to believe the best of others. It abides in hope and endures when all else fails. It is a life-long challenge.

LUKE, BOOK OF

The third book of the N.T., the Gospel of Luke, was intended as a defense of the historical data regarding Jesus – especially on behalf of the Greeks. Authored by Luke, a Gentile physician (Col. 4:14), it places considerable emphasis on Heaven's interest in the Gentiles. It also stresses the human side of the Lord (it records eleven of his prayers). The phrase "Son of man" is found twenty-six times in this book. In addition to being deity, Christ is the perfect man who came to seek and save the lost (19:10). Luke also authored the book of Acts. His credibility as a reliable historian is unreproached.

LXX

Roman numeral; seventy. Common abbreviation for the Greek Version of the O.T. (third century B.C.). See SEPTUAGINT.

MALACHI, BOOK OF

Malachi is the last prophet of the O.T. record. In the final era of O.T. history (mid to late fifth century B.C.), the people of God fell into a state of spiritual lethargy. They were insensitive, immoral, and inactive. There was corruption among the priests and among the people. Though the temple had been rebuilt, religious duties were neglected egregiously. The prophet blisters these people with a series of penetrating questions (some twenty three in this brief, four-chapter book). The narrative concludes with a prophecy of the work of John the Baptizer.

MAN

The Greek term for "man" is *anthropos*. Plato suggested that the word reflects the idea of an "upward looking" one, hinting, perhaps, that man finds no rest upon this planet. He is ever searching for his Maker. The term "man" is used generically – for human kind. "Let us make man in our image ... male and female created he them" (Gen. 1:26-27; cf. 6:3). Then, more specifically, "man" is used of the male of the species. "And Jehovah God called unto the man, and said unto him..." (Gen. 3:9, 20; 4:1). The question: "What is man?" (Psa. 8:4), has intrigued humanity since the dawn of time. Skepticism answers that he is but a freak of nature, the product of time and chance. All of the rational evidence points elsewhere. Man is a composite of body, soul, and spirit (1 Thes. 5:23). Each of these components deserves consideration. (a) Man's body is that which is material. The magnificent intricacy and orchestration argues for creative design, thus a designer (cf. Psa. 94:9; 139:14-15; 1 Cor. 12:18). Dr. William Beck of Harvard authored a textbook on anatomy/physiology which he appropriately titled, **Human Design**. That title speaks more than the author intended. (b) The human being is possessed of "soul" (*psuche*) as well. The term "soul" is used in varying ways in Scripture. Frequently it stands for the entire person (Ex. 1:5; 1 Pet. 3:20). Sometimes "soul" refers to the biological life within a physical organism – that which man shares in common with animals (Gen. 1:30; Mt. 2:20; Lk. 12:22). On the other hand, "soul" may be used of the eternal aspect of man, that which survives the death of the physical body (Mt. 10:28; Lk. 21:19; 1 Pet. 2:11; 3 Jn. 2; Rev. 6:9). (c) Man also has a "spirit" (*pneuma*) which resides within him, and without which he is dead (Lk. 8:55; Jas. 2:26). At the point of death, the spirit returns to the Creator who will deal with it justly (Eccl. 12:7). While "soul" and "spirit" are at times used interchangeably, mostly it is "spirit" that stands for the "inner man" (2 Cor. 4:16), that imperishable element of the human being that was created in the very image of God (Gen. 1:26). The spirit is that which has emotion (Dan. 7:15; Lk. 2:47; 1 Cor. 16:18) and intellect (1 Cor. 4:11). Three questions have ever been supreme for human consideration: (a) Whence our origin? The answer is: God. (b) What is our purpose? Atheism says: "We have none." Scripture affirms: "To reverence God and keep his commandments" (Eccl. 12:13; cf. Isa. 43:7). (c) What is the destiny of humanity? Either "at home with the Lord" (2 Cor. 5:8; Phil. 1:23) in heaven (Mt. 6:19; 2 Tim. 4:18), or for ever estranged from the Creator (Mt. 7:23; 2 Thes. 1:9) in GEHENNA (see).

MARK, BOOK OF

Mark's account of the life of Christ begins with the Savior's baptism. It is primarily directed to the Romans, one of the major cultures of the first century. It is designed to emphasize the actions of Jesus, more than his teaching. The Lord is represented as "the servant" of God, who does his Father's will with the greatest of urgency. A key word is "straightway" (immediately), used some forty times. This Gospel record gives considerable emphasis to the emotions of Christ.

MARRIAGE

Marriage is a covenant between a man and woman, whereby they pledge to belong to one another in a life-long union. There are several elements relative to this institution that are important to understand. (a) The *origin* of marriage is divine, commencing from the sixth day of the creation week (Gen. 2:24;

Mt. 19:5; Eph. 5:31). Man and woman, therefore, must respect God's regulations relative to the institution. (b) The *purpose* of marriage is manifold. The marital union (the home) is the cement that holds society together; it provides the ideal climate for the rearing of children, etc. Moreover, it provides human beings with a legitimate means of satisfying the sexual desire, if they are so inclined (1 Cor. 7:1ff). It is the means of man's greatest earthly happiness. Any assault upon the integrity of this institution undermines the stability of the human family at large. Additionally, this domestic unit facilitates the ideal environment for the spread of the gospel. This establishes a strong rationale for the preservation of its sanctity. (c) The *regulations* regarding marriage have been divinely imposed and may not be altered by civil adjudication. Marriage was designed as a heterosexual arrangement (cf. Rom. 1:26-27; 1 Cor. 6:9-10; Jude 7), involving one man and one woman (monogamous), abiding in the relationship for life (Gen. 2:24; Rom. 7:2; contrast 4:19). Though God tolerated a laxness toward the marriage relationship during a time of incomplete revelation (Mt. 19:8; Acts 14:16; 17:30), such permissiveness is given no license under the new and better covenant (Heb. 8:6). Jesus restored marriage to its original status (Mt. 19:8). Under the new covenant, the only cause for a second marriage is due to the death of one's spouse (Rom. 7:2-3; 1 Cor. 7:39), or the remarriage of an innocent victim who has left a union breached by fornication (Mt. 5:32; 19:9).

MARY

Mary was a Hebrew maiden who was chosen to be the mother of Jesus Christ. Her miraculous conception was prophesied in the O.T. (Isa. 7:14). Mary was certainly worthy of honor as a godly Jewish woman (see Mt. 1:16ff; Lk. 1:27ff; Jn. 19:25ff), but the cult-like superstition that has evolved regarding her, being promoted principally by the Roman Catholic Church, is foreign to the Scriptures. Several false doctrines related to Mary are a part of Catholic dogma. (a) It is alleged that Mary remained a virgin perpetually. She did not (Mt. 1:25; 12:46; 13:55-56; Jn. 2:12). (b) Catholics maintain that Mary was conceived "immaculately," i.e., free from "original sin," and that she remained sinless forever. The dogma is not true. Mary confessed her need for a *Savior* (Lk. 1:47). (c) Catholicism alleges that when Mary died, her body experienced no corruption; rather, three days following her demise, she was taken bodily into heaven, there to be crowned "Queen of Heaven." Though Catholic writers concede that this teaching "cannot be proved from the Bible," it became official dogma, that Catholics must believe, on November 1, 1950. (d) Catholic doctrine alleges that Mary is a "Mediatrix," between Christians and Christ, and that she is the "dispenser of graces" by the power of the Holy Spirit, based upon the merits of her crucified Son. No such position is sanctioned in the N.T. Christ is the "one mediator" between God and man (1 Tim. 2:5).

MATERIALISM

"Materialism" is commonly used in two different senses. (a) *Philosophical materialism* is the idea that nothing exists except that which is material in nature (i.e., composed of matter). There is, therefore, no spiritual Being known as "God" (Jn. 4:24). Moreover, man, according to this view, does not possess a "soul" or "spirit." He is totally a material being. When his body dies, his existence is over. This philosophy is terribly inadequate to explain so many things. For example, it cannot explain the origin of the Universe. Since the Universe is not eternal, and inasmuch as no material thing has the ability to create itself, materialism is left with no explanation as to its genesis. Materialism cannot explain the numerous traits unique to mankind, e.g., a sense of right and wrong, emotions like love, compassion, or a sense of esthetics, e.g., beauty. Materialism is a cold, dark ideology with no logic or comfort. (b) *Practical materialism* is the attempt to find lasting satisfaction in material things. It reflects a lifestyle wherein one lives *as if* there is nothing but matter. It finds an expression in covetousness, greed, slavish ambition to get ahead, unconcern for the needs of others, etc. (see Mt. 6:19ff; Lk. 12:15ff; 16:19ff). This ideology ignores the reality that the material is temporal, while the non-material is eternal (2 Cor. 4:18).

MATTHEW, BOOK OF

The book of Matthew is especially directed to Jews (hence, the heavy appeal to the O.T.). It is designed to demonstrate that Jesus of Nazareth was the fulfillment of the Messianic prophecies of the O.T. The apostle cites nearly forty O.T. predictions that were fulfilled by Jesus. He emphasizes that Christ was the "son of David," which was consistent with the Hebrew expectation (2 Sam. 7:12-13). Matthew gives great emphasis to Jesus' rebuke of the corrupt Jewish leaders, who would be instrumental in putting him to death (cf. chapter 23). He foretells the replacement of old Israel with a new, spiritual nation (21:43).

MEDIATOR

A "mediator" is a "go-between" (from *mesos*, "middle" and *eimi* "to go"). Ideally, the role of a mediator is to work for the reconciliation of parties that have become estranged. (a) Moses was a mediator between God and Israel. He delivered the law to the nation on behalf of Jehovah (Jn. 1:17; Gal. 3:19). At times he pled to the Lord on behalf of his wayward people (Ex. 32:32). (b) In a sense the prophets and priests of the old covenant functioned as mediators. The Hebrews did not approach God directly in worship; rather, they worshipped through a priestly group. Too, God did not put his revelation into the minds of each Jew. The Lord spoke through the prophets. (c) The ultimate and richest fulfillment of the role of a mediator was by Christ. The Lord's role as mediator was hinted at centuries before his incarnation (cf. Job 9:32-34), and it is developed fully in the New Testament (cf. 1 Tim. 2:5; Heb. 8:6; 9:15; 12:24). There are two points about Jesus' office as mediator that are of paramount significance. First, being both divine and human (Jn. 1:1, 14), he was equally related to the parties of estrangement – the Holy God on the one hand, and sinful man on the other. Second, by his perfect life and atoning death, he satisfied the justice of God (Isa. 53:11; Rom. 3:26), and was enabled to offer salvation to those who would obey him (Heb. 2:14ff; 5:8-9).

MESSIAH

The word "Messiah" is of O.T. origin. It derives from a Hebrew term meaning to "anoint." It becomes a special title that applies to Jesus of Nazareth. See: ANOINT, CHRIST.

MICAH, BOOK OF

Micah lived south of Jerusalem during the reigns of Jothan, Ahaz, and Hezekiah (cir. 749-697 B.C.). He was a contemporary of both Hosea and Isaiah. Micah's mission was to rebuke the sins of both Israel and Judah, and to foretell the punishing judgments that were to be visited upon them. He also depicts some of the glories of the coming Messianic age (2:12ff; 4:1ff; 5:2).

MILLENNIUM

The term "millennium" signifies a period of 1,000 years. It is a common belief among many who are identified with "Christendom" that Jesus Christ will return to this earth to set up his kingdom in the city of Jerusalem, there to reign for a span of one thousand years – called the "millennium." This theory is barren of Bible support. Note the following facts: (a) The basis of the doctrine of millennialism is asserted to be found in Revelation 20:1ff. It is not said to be expressed *anywhere else* in Scripture – which fact of itself makes it a most unlikely candidate for a major theological doctrine. (b) Revelation 20 lacks all of the major ingredients for the millennial dogma. There is no mention of Christ's return to earth, no allusion to David's throne, no mention of Jerusalem, no reference to the kingdom. (c) The term "thousand" (*chilias*) is found nineteen times in the book of Revelation; not once is it employed in a *literal* sense. (d) The "millennial" doctrine contradicts the general teaching of the Bible in numerous particulars. See DISPENSATIONALISM. (e) While the symbolism of Revelation is difficult at times, and there is some disagreement among responsible expositors, any view entertained with reference to particular points must be consistent with scriptural teaching elsewhere.

The most likely view of the "thousand years" is that it reflects a picture of the "complete" victory of the church over her enemies. This harmonizes with the general thrust of the book – Christ and his people overcome Satan and his forces (Rev. 20: 1ff; 14:1ff; 19:11-16).

MINISTER

There are three basic words in the Greek N.T. that convey the idea of "ministering" in one way or another. (a) *Diakonos*, occurs about thirty times in the N.T. Generally it simply means "to serve." In the KJV it is rendered "servant" seven times and "minister" twenty times. Three times it is used in the more technical sense of "deacon." See: DEACON. (b) The term *huperetes* literally meant "under rower," which originally suggested the servant who rowed the boat. It is found twenty times in the N.T. In the KJV it is rendered "officer" eleven times, "minister" five times, and "servant" four times. It suggests the idea of serving under another, as Mark did for Barnabas and Paul during a portion of the latter's first missionary campaign (Acts 13:5). (c) *Leitourgos* originally was one who voluntarily served the state at his own expense. It then came to take on the meaning of a specialized religious service. It is used only five times in the N.T. In Romans 13:6 it refers to government officials who "minister" to God, keeping order in society. It is used of the service of angels (Heb. 1:7), of Christ as he ministers before God in the heavenly sanctuary (Heb. 8:2), and of Paul and Epaphroditus, serving God in their respective capacities (Rom. 15:16; Phil. 2:25). In a generic sense, anyone who serves Christ is a minister of the Lord.

MIRACLE

Three Greek terms in the N.T. reflect the idea of a "miracle," and there are three contexts in which all three terms are found together (Acts 2:22; 2 Thes. 2:9; Heb. 2:4). The Greek terms are as follows. (a) *Dunamis* is "power, a mighty work." This word stresses the divine *power* involved in the miraculous event. (b) *Teras* is "a wonder." It describes the *effect* produced in those who observe, i.e., amazement is generated in their minds. (c) *Semeion* is a "sign." It indicates that the supernatural event is not an *end* within itself; rather it points to something else. In the case of the miracles performed by Christ and his apostles, the "signs" pointed to the fact that their messages were from God (cf. Jn. 3:2). A miracle is the exercise of the power of God whereby a natural law is temporarily suspended at a particular place for the purpose of establishing divine authority. Miracles were self-authenticating phenomena that could not be denied reasonably (Jn. 11:47; Acts 4:14, 16); they were rationalized superficially by the enemies of truth (Mt. 12:24). A careful study of the *nature* of the miracles recorded in the N.T. reveals they cannot be explained in any *naturalistic* way; they were subject to sense perception and were independent of secondary causes. Miracles were immediate and complete (Mk. 10: 52; Acts 3:7). They were publicly performed, and no base motives were detected in connection with them (Jn. 6:10; Acts 3:6). Miracles were *temporary* demonstrations of divine power while the revelatory process was in progress (Mk. 16:20; Heb, 2:3-4). When the N.T. documents were completed, miracles ceased (1 Cor. 13:8ff). See PROVIDENCE.

MISHNAH

See TALMUD.

NAHUM, BOOK OF

Under the preaching of Jonah, the wicked city of Nineveh had repented (Jon. 3:10; Mt. 12:40-41), and God had suspended the punishment of which he had warned those people. Eventually, though, they slipped back into their godless ways (3:1), and the time came when they would see their "full end," i.e., total destruction (1:8-9). God used Nahum to warn the Assyrians of their impending doom. The prophet vividly describes their catalog of sins and proclaims, on behalf of God: "I am against you!" Nineveh was destroyed in 612 B.C. So complete was the destruction that the city was "hid" (3:11) until the ruins were discovered finally in 1843.

NAME

The Greek term *onoma* takes on a very important place in the N.T. (a) Sometimes, by a figure known as metonymy, *the name stands for the person himself.* To trust in the Lord's name is to trust the Lord (Mt. 12:21). When one blasphemes God's name (Rev. 13:6), he has blasphemed God. (b) The term "name" is employed to stress the concept of *authority.* When a man cast out demons in Jesus' name, he was doing that act by the Lord's authority. To be immersed "in the name of Jesus Christ" (Acts 2:38) is to be immersed by Jesus' authority. Note also that, according to this passage, a baptism "for the remission of sins" is the only baptism *authorized* by the Savior. One is not to teach or practice anything in religion that is not authorized (either generically or specifically) by the authority of Christ (Col. 3:17). (c) Whenever the term "name" is used with the Greek preposition *eis,* i.e., "into the name," the sense is to *become the possession of* or to *come into fellowship with* the object of that name (1 Cor. 1:13, 15). Accordingly, when one is "baptized into the name of the Father, and of the Son, and the of the Holy Spirit" (Mt. 28:19), he becomes the *possession* of the Godhead and enters into full *fellowship* with the sacred three. There is no specific name (or names) that must be invoked audibly at the time of one's immersion. To use the expression "in the name of" describes what is being *done*, not what is being *said*.

NEHEMIAH, BOOK OF

This book contains the inspired record of Israel's final return from the Babylonian captivity. The leader of the trek was Nehemiah, who brought the Hebrews back in 444 B.C. It is the story of the rebuilding of Jerusalem's walls in a time of great discouragement. Though the people had been zealous in the days of Ezra (about a dozen years earlier), they were despondent again. The Jews were persecuted by their enemies and the city walls were in a state of disarray. Nehemiah becomes governor and leads the people to a state of renewal.

NEW BIRTH

This expression takes its rise from the language employed by Christ in his conversation with Nicodemus (Jn. 3:1ff). The facts regarding the "new birth" are these. (a) It is an absolutely *essential* requirement for entering the kingdom of God. Jesus said that "except" one is born "anew" he cannot enter the kingdom (vv. 3, 5); the conditions of the new birth involve a process that one "must" do in order to please God (v. 7). (b) The birth process consists of *two phases*. First, there is the role of the *Spirit*. The work of the Holy Spirit is analogous to that of a father. The divine Spirit is the author of the word of God

(1 Cor. 2:11ff; Eph. 6:17), which, figuratively speaking, is the "seed" by which the state of "belief" is generated within the sinner's heart (cf. Lk. 8:11; 1 Cor. 4:15; Jas. 1:18; 1 Pet. 1:22-23). Second, there is the role of *water.* Water clearly is an allusion to baptism; modern attempts to deny this fact (which date back only to the time of John Calvin) have been futile. Note the logic: The "new birth" (containing water) puts one into God's kingdom (Jn. 3:3, 5). But the kingdom is the church (Mt. 16:18-19). Thus the "new birth" admits one into the church. Since the church is also the body of Christ (Eph. 1:22-23; Col. 1:18, 24), one must conclude that the new birth introduces one into the body. This conclusion parallels the proposition that "by one Spirit" one is *"baptized* into one body" (1 Cor. 12:13). The "water" of John 3:5 is, therefore, obviously the equivalent of "baptized" in the Corinthian passage (see also Eph. 5:26; Tit. 3:5).

NEW TESTAMENT

The New Testament is a collection of twenty-seven documents: (a) They are classified as "scripture," a term suggesting a divine writing (1 Tim. 5:18; 2 Pet. 3:16). (b) Eight known writers – Matthew, Mark, Luke, John, Paul, Peter, James, and Jude – produced these books. (c) The time of composition covered approximately fifty years. The final book, Revelation, was completed about A.D. 96. (d) The first four books are *biographical* in design, providing select details of the life of Christ. Acts is a *history* of the growth of the early church. Romans through Jude are *instructional letters* to churches and individual Christians. Revelation is *prophetic* in content, showing the ultimate victory of truth over error. (e) The value of the N.T. is in the fact that it shows that the promised Messiah was manifested in Jesus of Nazareth, who is the Son of God. It reveals the establishment of his church and its explosive growth in the first-century world. It provides instruction as to how one becomes a Christian and how he remains faithful in his service to God. It bestows confidence in the final triumph of God's plan over the evil forces of the world.

NUMBERS, BOOK OF

The fourth book of the Pentateuch, Numbers, derives its title from the fact that a census of the Israelite people was taken after they had departed from Egypt. There were some 603,550 men, above the age of twenty who were capable of military combat (Num. 1:46), which may suggest an overall population of two to three million souls. The book covers most of that period of time when the Israelites wandered in the wilderness of Sinai, approximately thirty-eight years and nine months. The wilderness sojourn was a result of the Hebrews' lack of faith in God's power to deliver them, when they spied out the land of Canaan (Num. 14:32-34).

OBADIAH, BOOK OF

The descendants of Esau (brother of Jacob) were the Edomites. They were a people who settled in the region to the southeast of Palestine. They became a tribe that was very hostile to the Israelite people, providing comfort to the Hebrews' enemies on occasion. They felt very secure in their cliff-top dwellings, but God warned that he would bring them down. Other nations were also warned of impending judgment by the prophet.

OBEY

The English word "obey" translates both Hebrew and Greek words that express parallel ideas – that of listening, being attentive to someone who possesses authority. Thus, the words suggest an active response to instruction, not merely awareness of sound. Note: "Then [Moses] took the book of the covenant, and read it in the hearing of the people; and they said, 'All that the Lord has spoken we will do, and we will be obedient'" (Ex. 24:7 RSV). In the N.T., the Greek word for "obey" is *hupakouo*, literally, to "hear under." This pictures the student, under the teacher's authority, listening with a view to obedience. Obedience proceeds from: (a) being exposed to the message; (b) having confidence in the integrity of the message; (c) believing the instruction; and, (d) accepting responsibility for yielding to its demands. Obedience must be: (a) from the heart (Rom. 6:17), i.e., sincerely offered – not out of false motives; (b) completely rendered – partial obedience is *no* obedience (see 1 Sam. 15:1-23). Obedience is doing *what* the Lord prescribed, in the *manner* authorized, and for the *purpose* specified. Christ is the Author of salvation to the obedient, not the disobedient (Heb. 5:8-9; see Jn. 3:36 ASV). Obedience is required of: (a) men to God (Acts 5:29); (b) citizens to civil authorities (Rom. 13:1); (c) children to parents (Eph. 6:1); (d) Christians to church elders (Heb. 13:17); (e) wives to husbands (Eph. 5:22ff); (f) and employees to employers (Eph. 6:5ff). All subordinate levels of obedience must be regulated by the supreme will of God (Acts 4:19; 5:28-29).

OLD TESTAMENT

The Old Testament is the Hebrew Bible – a collection of thirty-nine books. (a) These books are inspired of God (Mt. 22:31-32;

2 Tim. 3:15-17). (b) The documents were produced over a period of about 1,000 years, being authored by some thirty or so writers. (c) There are four major divisions of the O.T. These are: *Law* (the first five books), *History* (the next twelve books), *Poetry* (Job through Song of Solomon), *Prophecy* (the last seventeen books). (d) These documents span that era from the creation of the Universe down to the time the Hebrew people are delivered from Babylonian captivity. (e) The thrust of the O.T. is to demonstrate the development of God's plan of redemption, as such was worked out through the Jewish people and their interaction with other nations. O.T. history is, therefore, highly selective. (f) The value of the O.T. is seen in: its *preparation* for the coming of Christ (Gal. 3:24), its *great moral lessons* that are timeless (Rom. 15:4; 1 Cor. 10:6, 11), its cultivation of an *awareness of the nature of sin* (Rom. 7:7, 13). (g) The Old Covenant, as a binding legal system, was restricted to the nation of Israel (Dt. 5:1-5), and was abrogated with the death of Christ on the cross (Gal. 3:25; Eph. 2:11ff; Col. 2:14ff).

PANTHEISM

This word derives from the Greek – *pan* ("all") and *theos* ("God"). Traditionally, the term reflects a religious theory that suggests the entire Universe is endued with the *nature of God*. God is not only everywhere (omnipresent), *everything*, in reality, *is* "God." This ideology, which permeates the so-called New Age philosophy so popular today, effectually denies the existence of a personal God apart from his creation. Actually, it is a form of idolatry (see Rom. 1:25).

PARADISE

The Greek word *paradeisos* derives from the Persian term *pairidaeza*, which meant an enclosure, a royal park, a garden with a wall. In the Greek Old Testament (LXX) the term is employed of the garden of Eden (Gen. 2:8; cf. Ezek. 31:8). Paradise is found three times in the N.T. (a) While hanging on the cross, Jesus promised the penitent robber that the two of them would be together in Paradise later that day (Lk. 23:43). The reference is to that intermediate state of the righteous dead, that precedes the final day and the resurrection of the body. (b) In 2 Corinthians 12:4, Paul alludes to an experience earlier in his ministry, at which time he was caught up "into Paradise" (2 Cor. 12:4). There is a difference of opinion among scholars as to whether or not this is the intermediate state or heaven itself. Some argue that it is the same as heaven; others note the distinction between *heno*s ("as far as" the third heaven) and *eis* ("into" Paradise), thus suggesting that the intermediate state is here referenced, as in Luke 23:43. (c) In Revelation 2:7, the place of the "tree of life," i.e., heaven itself (cf. 22:2), is designated as Paradise and is promised to those who remain faithful to the Lord. Late Jewish literature distinguished between the "first" Paradise (Eden), the "hidden" Paradise (Lk. 23:43; 2 Cor. 12:4), and heaven itself (Rev. 2:7). One must remember that a word can take on different senses, depending upon the context in which it is found.

PEACE

The Greek word *eirene* ("peace") may derive from an original term meaning, "to weave together." This is a very significant Bible word. (a) There is a peace to be sought *with God*. Sin has separated man from his Creator (Isa. 59:1-2), so that rebellious

Bible Words and Theological Terms Made Easy

man has become an enemy to God (Rom. 5:10; Jas. 4:4). But the "God of peace" (1 Thes. 5:23) has provided an avenue of reconciliation so that union with him may be enjoyed once more. The shedding of Christ's blood was the price of peace (Eph. 2:13-14, 17; Col. 1:20). That message is revealed in the "gospel of peace" (Eph. 6:15). Peace is enjoyed by the exercise of "faith," and is focused in that realm that is designated as being "in Christ." This state is entered when one's obedience is consummated at the point of baptism (Rom. 6:3-4; Gal. 3:26-27). (b) Obedience to the truth of the gospel brings the Christian an *inner peace* that is inexplicable from the human vantagepoint. It passes all understanding and guards our hearts and thoughts in Christ Jesus (Phil. 4:7). (c) There is also the peace that should exist *between all men*, who are the "offspring" of God (Acts 17:28). Christians must lead the way in this quest for peace. They are to be the "peace-makers" (Mt. 5:8). The children of God are to be at peace among themselves (1 Thes. 5:13; 2 Tim. 2:22), and they are to attempt to be at peace with all others (Rom. 12:18; Heb. 12:14). The Lord's people, therefore, should remain aloof from the carnal conflicts of this world (Jn. 18:36; Eph. 6:12; 2 Cor. 10:4ff; 2 Tim. 2:24).

PENTECOST, DAY OF

The day of Pentecost was an annual Jewish festival which came fifty days (the word signifies "fiftieth") after the Passover celebration (Lev. 23:15-21; Dt. 16:9-12). It was known also as the feast of weeks (Ex. 34:22), the feast of harvest (Ex. 23:16), or the feast of first fruits (Num. 28:26). It always fell on the day following the Sabbath, hence, on Sunday. It was on the day of Pentecost, fifty days following the death of Christ, that the apostles were empowered with the Holy Spirit. The gospel was preached in all its fullness and the Lord's kingdom was established. On that day the "first fruits" of Christianity were gleaned, which was a preview of the vast "harvest" to follow (see Acts 2:1ff).

PERFECT

The word "perfect" is used in different ways in the Bible. (a) Only deity (Father, Son, and Holy Spirit) is perfect in the absolute, moral sense (Mt. 5:48), though Christians are to strive for this quality. Whenever man is referred to as "perfect" it is only in a *relative* sense, i.e., he is spiritually mature, in comparison to his fellows (Job. 1:1; cf. Phil. 3:12ff). (b) Sometimes "perfect" is employed in the sense of completeness. Jesus, by his suffering, became completely qualified to serve as our High Priest (Heb. 5:8-9). The Scriptures furnish the man of God to the end that he may be "perfect" (KJV), i.e., completely furnished (ASV), for the Christian life (2 Tim. 3:17). In 1 Corinthians 13:8ff, Paul speaks of the cessation of miraculous gifts. The target time for the termination of those phenomena would be "when that which is perfect" is come. The Greek text literally speaks of "the perfect thing" (neuter gender) to come. Here, "perfect" means "complete," and it is placed in contrast to the "in part" things, i.e., the bit-by-bit revelatory process that was conveyed by means of the various spiritual gifts (see 12:7ff). The "perfect," or "complete," revelation was realized when the N.T. record was finished (cir. A.D. 96).

PETER 1, BOOK OF

Peter addressed this letter to "the elect," i.e., Christians, who are dispersed in Asia Minor. The main theme of the epistle is explicitly stated. He urges the brethren to "stand fast" in the "grace of God" (5:12). The apostle appeals to these Christians to maintain courage, to be pure, and to remain loyal to Christ. He exhorts the saints to live lives that correspond to the gospel (1:13-2:10). He urges them to yield to God's sovereignty as manifested in the world's affairs (2:13ff). Saints are encouraged in view of the suffering they must endure (3:13-5:11).

PETER 2, BOOK OF

Peter's second letter is a caustic warning regarding false teachers who are promoting "destructive heresies" (2:1). The false teaching concerns the nature of Christ, sensual indulgence, the coming of Christ, and the end of the world. Appealing heavily to O.T. history, he shows by multiple examples that the child of God is not eternally secure. Rather, Christians must "grow in the grace and knowledge" of Christ (3:18). Their goal is the "eternal kingdom" (1:11).

PHILEMON, BOOK OF

Philemon was a Christian who lived in the city of Colossae. Philemon owned a slave whose name was Onesimus. Onesimus fled to Rome where he came in contact with, and was converted by, Paul. The apostle sends Onesimus back to his master bearing this letter, urging Philemon to receive the runaway back, as a "brother" in the Lord. The subtle message of the epistle contains the seeds for the abolition of the evil institution of slavery.

PHILIPPIANS, BOOK OF

The Philippian church was established by Paul on his first missionary journey (Acts 16:11ff). These people quickly secured a place in the great apostle's heart. This letter, written some ten years after the founding of the congregation, is designed to thank them for their support in the gospel all these years. It is also an appeal to these brothers to stay united, because there were threats to peace from without and within the church. Too, it offers a word of commendation on behalf of Epaphroditus, a helper of Paul's from the city of Philippi, who had been ill and was being sent home. It is a letter of great love and joy.

PRAISE

Praise, in the highest sense of the term, is a feeling toward, and/or outward expression of, devotion to deity. It acknowledges thanksgiving for Heaven's glorious creation, beneficent providence, and redemptive mercy (cf. Ex. 15:1-19; Rev. 4:8, 11; 5:9, 12-13). Deity, because of his very nature, is worthy to be praised (Psa. 18:3). Praise to God may be public or private (Psa. 96:3). In the O.T. era, God was praised in various forms, e.g., with musical instruments, in dance (Psa. 150:3-4), in song (66:1-2), and with burnt offerings (66:13-15). But under the N.T. regime, there is no authority for either the instruments, the dance, or burnt offerings. One may praise God in prayer or in song, but the carnal trappings of the Mosaic economy are now obsolete (Col. 2:14ff; Heb. 9:1-10).

PRAYER

Prayer is a mode of communication between a human being and deity. Prayer is almost a human "instinct," reflecting man's innate need for contact with his Maker (Acts 17:27). It has been said that when one realizes that he is "lost," he cannot help praying. While that may well be true, the Bible promises the power of effectual prayer only under certain conditions. (a) Prayer is an avenue of communication between a child of God and his/her heavenly Father (Mt. 6:9). But one becomes a child of God by means of the "new birth" process (Jn. 3:3-5). Prayer is thus a spiritual privilege for those who are "in Christ" (Jn. 15:7; Eph. 1:3). The Creator does not hear those whose lives are in rebellion (Prov. 28:9; 1 Pet. 3:12). The first rule for prayer is that one must have a proper relationship with the Lord. Saul of Tarsus prayed for three days, but his sins were not washed away until he obeyed the gospel (Acts 9:11; 22:16). (b) One must have confidence in the validity of prayer. The person who prays in doubt receives nothing (Jas. 1:5-8; cf. Mt. 21:22). (c) Prayer must be persistent (1 Thes. 5:17). Men ought always to pray, and not to faint (Lk. 18:1). Thus we must keep on asking, seeking, and knocking (Lk. 11:9), and let God answer in his own time and in his own way (2 Cor. 12:8-9). Paul prayed that he might go to Rome (Rom. 1:10), yet it was some three years before his request was granted (Acts 28). (d) Prayer must be accompanied by a genuinely spiritual life. The Lord's words must abide in you (Jn. 15:7), for it is the prayer of the righteous that avails much (Jas. 5:16; 1 Pet. 3:12; cf. 1 Tim. 2:8; 1 Pet. 3:7). It is hypocritical to want to talk with God while one is flagrantly living for Satan. (e) Prayer must be offered in harmony with the revealed will of God (1 Jn. 5:14). One cannot pray for God to reduce his age by twenty years, for that would involve a miracle and Heaven is not providing miracles today (1 Cor. 13:

A Practical Handbook

8ff). It is not appropriate to pray that Jehovah will save (independent of the divine plan) some hardened rebel who refuses to obey the gospel plan. Proper procedure for prayer must be "learned" (Lk. 11:1). It is up to Christians to research the "rules" of acceptable prayer.

PREDESTINATION
See ELECT.

PRIEST
A priest is one who offers sacrifice and ministers in services pertaining thereto (cf. Heb. 5:1). This term implies recognition of sin and the need for atonement, in some fashion or another. (a) The term is used of pagan priests who sacrificed to false gods (Acts 14:13). (b) In the earliest age of human history (Patriarchal period), the father of each family served as priest, offering sacrifices on behalf of his people (Gen. 8:20; Job 1:5). Melchizedek, a contemporary of Abraham, was not only a king, he was a priest as well (Gen. 14:18). (c) During the Mosaic era, a special priesthood of the family of Aaron (Moses' brother) was appointed by God; those priests, divided into twenty-four orders (1 Chron. 24:4ff), served on a rotating basis (cf. Lk. 1:8-9). (d) With the termination of the law of Moses (Col. 2:14ff), the priesthood system was changed (Heb. 7:12). By virtue of the shedding of his blood, at the time of his ascension Christ entered heaven to function as a high priest for the people of God (Heb. 4:15; 5:5, 15, etc.). He is a "great high priest" (Heb. 4:14), who, after the order of Melchizedek, is a king as well (Psa. 110; Heb. 5:10). (e) Under the administration of Christ, all Christians are priests (1 Pet. 2:5, 9; Rev. 1:5, etc.) who offer

their own sacrifices in worship (Rom. 12:1; Phil. 2:17; Heb. 13:15); they need no *physical* priesthood to stand between them and God. There are several ideas in the modern community of "Christendom" that are erroneous. (a) Both Roman Catholic and Mormon theology allow for an unauthorized physical priesthood. (b) The "dispensational" theory alleges that the Levitical priesthood will be "resumed, nationally, on behalf of Gentiles, in the Millennial Kingdom" (W.E. Vine). This idea has no biblical support.

PROPITIATION

There are three kindred words in the Greek N.T. that represent the idea of "propitiation." Two are nouns – *hilasmos* (1 Jn. 2:2; 4:10) and *hilasterion* (Rom. 3:25; Heb. 9:5), and the third is the verb *hilaskomai* (Lk. 18:13; Heb. 2:17). The terms are designed to provide an explanation as to how God, who is absolutely holy (Isa. 6:3; Hab. 1:13), can pardon sinful humanity (Rom. 3:10, 23), and still be accounted as just (Psa. 89:14). The answer is to be found in "Christ," the sinless offering (Jn. 1:29; 1 Pet. 1:19-20), who became the "propitiation" (Rom. 3:25), i.e., the "mercy-seat" (covering) for our transgressions (see Heb. 9:5 ASVfn). The Savior's atoning sacrifice is accessed when one yields to his will (Heb. 5:9) in obedience to the gospel plan of redemption (2 Thes. 1:8; Mk. 16:16; Acts 2:38). See JUSTICE, JUSTIFICATION.

PSALLO

The Greek word *psallo* is found five times in the N.T. It is rendered by the English terms "sing" (Rom. 15:9; 1 Cor. 14:15; Jas. 5:13), and "make melody" (Eph. 5:19). In the era of classical

Greek (cir. 900 to 330 B.C.), the word was used in the sense of "to touch" or "to twang," as with a carpenter's line or bow string. During the time of the Septuagint (Greek O.T. third century B.C.), the word was employed of singing (Psa. 135:3), playing an instrument (1 Sam. 16:16), or singing to the accompaniment of an instrument (Psa. 33:2) – the instrument being supplied by the context. In the N.T., however, the word is used only in the sense of singing. If the term *inheres* an instrument in Ephesians 5:19, then: (a) one cannot not *psallo* without using the instrument; (b) since each person is to *psallo* personally, each would have to play an instrument; (c) it would have to be an instrument capable of being "plucked." Perhaps this is why very few scholars in modern times are using the *"psallo"* argument in defense of instrumental music in Christian praise. The N.T. does not authorize the use of mechanical instruments for Christian worship.

PSALMS, BOOK OF

Psalms is a collection of 150 songs of praise, authored by a variety of writers (seventy-three are attributed to David). They celebrate the Lord's power of creation and his sovereignty over nature. The Psalms reflect an awareness of Israel's redemptive role in the history of mankind. A number of the songs in this wonderful book are Messianic in their thrust (see Psalm 2 and Psalm 22). This collection of poetic literature presents a portrait of man's doubts, fears, and aspirations. The Psalms forcefully direct our attention to the need of praising the Creator for his manifold works, and particularly his loving interest in humanity.

PROPHECY

"Prophecy" is a message from God; the act of bringing forth that message is "prophesying." "Prophecy" derives from a compound Greek term consisting of *pro* ("forth") and *phemi*, "to speak," hence, "to speak forth." (a) Most frequently in the Bible, prophecy, when used of righteous people, reflected a divine gift by which one brought a message from God. The message could focus on events that had *occurred already*. For instance, when Moses recorded the information relative to the creation of the Universe, he functioned as a "prophet" (cf. Dt. 18:15). He provided information that could not have been known naturally. Amos was acting in the role of a prophet when he spoke concerning *contemporary* conditions in Israel (Amos 1:1). Isaiah uttered *predictive* prophecy when he foretold marvelous things regarding the Messiah, who was to come centuries later (Isa. 53). Predictive prophecy is one of the amazing evidences of Bible inspiration. There are prophecies relating to: nations (Dan. 2), individuals (Isa. 44:28; 45:1), the coming Christ (Isa. 53), etc. (b) Occasionally, the term "prophesy" appears to be used simply in the sense of "teach" (2 Pet. 2:1 – note the connective "also" between "prophets" and "teachers"), or within a context of worship (1 Kgs. 18:29; 1 Cor. 11:4-5). The person who speaks forth words of edification, consolation, and exhortation – prophesies (1 Cor. 14:3), whether by inspiration or otherwise. (c) The Scriptures also warn of false prophets; these are those who feign to speak for God but do not (Mt. 7:16; cf. Tit. 1:12). Many, who claim to have spoken on behalf of the Lord, will hear him say – at the time of judgment: "I never knew you: depart from me, you that work iniquity" (Mt. 7:23).

PROVERBS, BOOK OF

The book of Proverbs is a collection of wise sayings, many of which were written by Solomon, king of Israel (cf. 1 Kgs. 4:32), and addressed to his son (presumably Rehoboam). The material within the book spans more than 200 years – at least to the days of Hezekiah (25:1). The proverbs are designed to instruct the young in principles of divine wisdom, such as can assist the godly in living a prudent life in a world saturated with evil. More than 100 times a form of the term "wise" is employed.

PROVIDENCE OF GOD

The word "providence," is not used explicitly of divine activity in the Scriptures, though the concept is apparent in both Testaments. The word basically means "foresight." Theologically, it has been coined to explain the operations of God in: (a) maintaining the created world (Neh. 9:6; Col. 1:17; Heb. 1:3); and, (b) Jehovah's workings among the nations of the world, and especially with his people, toward the successful realization of the plan for human redemption. There are several principles relative to providence that should be noted. (a) Whereas miracles reveal the *direct* operation of God, in the *suspension* of natural law, Providence *employs* these laws for the *indirect* implementation of the divine will. (b) Providence manipulates human events to a divine end, and yet, somehow, it preserves man's freedom of choice (cf. Isa. 10:5-7; Jer. 25:8-11). (c) Since providence is a "behind-the-scenes" mode of heavenly operation, one cannot identify specific instances of it with certainty (Esth. 4:14; Philem. 15), though he may confidently affirm that it occurs, because the Bible makes that matter quite clear (Gen. 45:5, 7; 50:20). See MIRACLE.

PURGATORY

Purgatory is a state, fabricated by the Roman Catholic Church, which is supposed to be a depository for those who die, not wicked enough to enter hell, but not good enough to merit heaven. These "sanctified," but flawed, Christians must enter "purgatory" where they remain until their sins are expiated, or, to say the same thing in another way, until they are "purged." Further, Catholic dogma contends that prayers may be made (and money paid) for those suffering in purgatory, thus, hastening their departure from that dreadful abode. The doctrine is false: (a) There is no mention of this dogma in Scripture. (b) It denies one's personal responsibility for sin, suggesting that others can help in expiating the punishment for disobedience (contra Rom. 14:12; cf. Ezek. 18:20b). (c) It implies that one, to some extent, atones for his own sin by his suffering. This is at variance with Paul's affirmation that we are not saved by meritorious works (Eph. 2:8-9) – either before or after death. (d) All preparation for eternity must be made before one dies (cf. Mt. 25:1-12). (e) The rich man in "hades" entertained no hope of escape, being separated from the abode of the righteous by a *permanent* (so the thrust of the perfect tense verb, "fixed") and impassible gulf (Lk. 16:26).

QUICKEN

This English term is a rendition of the Greek *zoopoieo*, "to make alive." It is found about a dozen times in the N.T. and is rendered by such expressions as "quicken," "give life," and "make alive." Consider these facts: (a) The power to "make alive" is always attributed either to God (Jn. 5:21; Rom. 4:17; 8:11) or to Christ (Jn. 5:21; 6:63; 1 Cor. 15:22, 45). This is strong testimony to the deity of Jesus. (b) God, by the act of creation, has "given life" to all things (1 Tim. 6:13; cf. Acts 17:25). (c) The word is used of granting life to one who has been spiritually dead (Eph. 2:1, 5; Col. 2:13 – In these latter two passages, *zoopoieo* has the prefix *sun*, "with," demonstrating that spiritual life is conferred only in connection with the work of Christ). Paul argues that the law of Moses could not confer this life (Gal. 3:21). (d) *Zoopoieo* is employed with reference to the bodily resurrection of Jesus (1 Pet. 3:18). (e) Finally, it signifies the reanimation of the human body at the time of the general resurrection (Rom. 8:11; 1 Cor. 15:36).

QUIET

The Greek noun *hesuchia* does not signify absolute silence, i.e., absence of sound, but that which is tranquil, causing no disturbance. When Paul addressed an unruly mob, and they perceived that he spoke in Hebrew, they "were the more quiet" (Acts 22:2). One might say they "idled down," as suggested by the verbal tense. They became more disposed to listen. In 1 Timothy 2:11-12, Paul admonishes that woman is to "learn in quietness." Moreover, she is not to "exercise authority" over man; rather, she is to possess a "quiet" spirit (cf. 1 Pet. 3:4, where the adjective *hesuchios*, "quiet," is coupled with "meek"). Several points must be made concerning this term. (a) This does not prohibit a woman speaking, in an appropriate manner, in a church service or elsewhere. (b) The instruction is not restricted to a church meeting. (c) It has to do with a woman's recognition of her relationship to man, whom God has appointed as her "head" (cf. 1 Cor. 11:3). (d) Paul's requirements are grounded in principles that extend back to the creation. They are *not,* therefore, culturally conditioned, and thus obsolete today.

RANSOM

Jesus once declared that he came to this earth to give up his life as a "ransom" for others (cf. Mt. 20:28; Mk. 10:45). The term for "ransom" is *lutron*. *Lutron* derives from *luo*, "to loose," and when the suffix is added, the meaning suggested is "the *means of loosing*." In the O.T., the word was used of the price paid for one's life (Ex. 21:30), or the redemption cost of a slave (Lev. 19: 20). In the context of the N.T., Christ becomes the price paid to redeem sinful man. In sin, one is separated from God (Isa. 59: 1-2), hence, dead (Eph. 2:1). The Lord's shed blood is a price that is able to remedy that condition by bestowing life (salvation). Also, by his personal choice to disobey God, man has "sold" himself into the bondage of sin (Jn. 8:34; Rom. 7:14); again, however, the Savior's death was the price of redemption (Eph. 1:6). In 1 Timothy 2:6, Paul affirms that Christ "gave himself a ransom [*antilutron*] for all...." The addition of *anti* ("instead of") to *lutron*, gives even greater emphasis to the substitutionary nature of Jesus death. Two important points must be emphasized in conclusion: (a) The death of Jesus was voluntary – he gave his life up for others. (b) Potentially, it was available for "all" (cf. "all men" and "all" – 1 Tim. 2:1, 4, 6). The Calvinistic doctrine of "limited atonement," i.e., that Jesus died only for *some* (the elect) is not in harmony with the Scriptures.

RAPTURE

This word derives from the Latin term *rapio*, "to snatch." The corresponding Greek expression is *harpazo*, signifying "caught up" (cf. 2 Cor. 12:2, 4) or "caught away" (Acts 8:39). At the time of Christ's return to raise the dead (Jn. 5:28-29; Acts 24:15), the Lord's people will be "caught up" to be with him evermore (1 Thes. 4:17). The wicked dead will also be raised, but they will appear before the Judge of the earth to receive their final sentence. The term "rapture" has become an important element in the dogma of DISPENSATIONALISM (see). This theory alleges that in the near future Jesus will return to "rapture" his saints (the wicked are said to remain in their graves). Supposedly, this rapture will occur in connection with a "seven year tribulation period." For some, the rapture will occur at the beginning of the "tribulation" period; for others, it will be at mid-point, or, at the end. This rapture, it is contended, will herald the 1,000-year reign of Christ upon the earth. This theory is unfounded, being based upon a misunderstanding of Revelation 20:1ff. In the same Thessalonian correspondence, the coming of Christ is treated as a single event, impacting both believers and unbelievers (2 Thes. 1:6-10). The "rapture" dogma was unknown prior to the early 1800's.

REASON

Reason is the intellectual ability of human beings to gather facts and from them draw correct conclusions. Reason is one of the traits of human kind that separates man from animals (cf. Jude 10). There are several abuses of "reason" that are worthy of special attention: (a) There is the arrogant view of "rationalism," the ideology that man, by the use of his own mind, is entirely capable of solving all his problems and managing his destiny. He therefore has no need for religion. This concept really exalts man to the status of being his own "god," and it has its roots in pagan Greek philosophy. (b) A second error is the notion that the Bible must be measured in the light of human reason and experience. If, therefore, a biblical event (e.g., the miraculous) does not conform to modern experience, it is assumed that it is not reasonable to believe that it occurred. Hence, it is rejected as historical reality. This has led certain theologians to attempt "surgery" upon the sacred text, removing all miraculous elements (e.g., Jesus' virgin birth, his miracles, the Lord's resurrection, etc.) from the realm of reality. This concept ignores historical evidence in deference to subjective assumption. (c) An equally fallacious view is the idea that faith must simply be "experienced" by a "blind leap into the dark" – that investigation, evidence, and deduction are irrelevant to establishing one's religious pursuits. Reason and logic are debunked, and "faith" becomes a "feel-good," venture into subjectivism. This view does not conform to the pattern of apostolic teaching. For example, following his conversion, Saul of Tarsus "confounded the Jews that dwelt at Damascus, proving that this Jesus is the Christ" (Acts 9:22). The term "proving" is the Greek *sumbibazo*, which means "to bring together." Paul appealed to O.T. prophecies, compared them with facts regarding Jesus, and drew the irresistible conclusion that Jesus of Nazareth was the Messiah. The Jews were unable to answer the apostle's logic. There is a legitimate use of "reason" in Christianity.

RECONCILE

The verb "reconcile" (Grk. *katallasso*) basically suggests a "change." In an ethical or religious sense, it denotes a change between parties who have been estranged. It may refer to *human* associations, or man's relationship to his *Creator*. (a) In human relationships that are breached, the fault may lie with one of the parties or with both. In Matthew 5:24 a case is contemplated where two brothers are estranged and need reconciliation. The Greek *diallasso* suggests that a mutual concession is needed to pacify a mutual hostility (Vine). If one finds it absolutely imperative to become separated from a spouse (where no sexual infidelity has been involved), he should either remain in a separated state, or else be "reconciled" to his mate (1 Cor. 7:11). (b) Human beings, by virtue of personal sins, have been *alienated from God* (cf. Eph. 2:12; 4:18; Col. 1:21). God is in no way responsible for the separation (Isa. 59:1-2); man is wholly culpable. However, Jehovah, as a result of his great love, has implemented a plan of reconciliation. It involved the death of his Son (Rom. 5:10; Col. 1:22), during which Jesus' blood was shed (Eph. 2:16; Col. 1:20). Christ, an innocent sacrifice, stands in for sinful man. All men are urged to accept Heaven's offer of reconciliation, which is made known through the gospel message (2 Cor. 5:18-19). The command "be ye reconciled to God" (2 Cor. 5:20), suggests that the sinner has the power to accept, if he but will (cf. Jn. 5:40; Rev. 22:17). Reconciliation is formalized at the point of the believing penitent being baptized into the body of Christ (Eph. 2:16; 1 Cor. 12:13; cf. Eph. 5:26).

REDEEMER

A "redeemer" is one who is qualified to effect "redemption" on behalf of one in need of the same. The term "redeem" means "to buy out of," (Grk. *exagorazo* – *ek* "out of" and *agorazo*, "buy"), as in the case of a slave who is bought out of the state of bondage. When Jehovah delivered his people from Egyptian slavery, it was a type of redemption (Ex. 6:6; 5:13; cf. Psa. 78:35). The Lord also promised to redeem Israel from her sins (Psa. 130:8; cf. Isa. 59:20; Rom. 11:26). Redemption reaches its richest meaning in the atoning work of Jesus Christ. (a) Job longed for a "Redeemer," and declared that he would come to earth someday (Job 19:25). (b) The Hebrew O.T. spoke of a *goel*, a kinsman with the right to redeem. Boaz, who married Ruth, is an example of such (Ruth 3-4). Christ, by his identification with humanity (Jn. 1:14), and his death at Calvary, became our "kinsman-Redeemer" (Lk. 1:68; Eph. 1:7). (c) Jesus redeemed the obedient Jew from the curse of the law of Moses, i.e., his inability to keep it perfectly, thus being subject to its penalty (Gal. 3:13; 4:5). God offered redemption by means of the plan involving the death of his Son (Rom. 3:24; 1 Cor. 1:30; 1 Pet. 1:18-19). (d) Eventually, at the time of his second coming, Christ will redeem the bodies of the dead from the grave (Rom. 8:23; Eph. 4:30).

REFORMATION

The Greek word for "reformation" is *diorthosis*, which indicates the idea of making something "straight." A kindred form of the term is used in Acts 24:2, where the flattering orator Tertullus described the political activity of Felix. Supposedly, the governor "corrected" evils that had been perpetrated against the Jews. Consider the following uses in both biblical and ecclesiastical history: (a) In the O.T. period, both Hezekiah and Josiah initiated reforms, after the Hebrew people had dredged themselves deeply into sin (2 Kgs. 18:1-8; 23:4-20). (b) More significantly, the term "reformation" is employed to depict the Christian regime (Heb. 9:10; cf. v. 9, "time present"), in contrast to the Mosaic economy. It describes the new order, Christianity, which was intended by God to replace the carnal system of Judaism. (c) In a more modern sense, "reformation" has reference to a religious effort that sought to correct the corruption that gradually had afflicted the "Christian" movement over the centuries (2 Thes. 2:1ff; 1 Tim. 4:1ff; 2 Tim. 4:

1ff), resulting ultimately in the development of the Roman Catholic Church. Though there were others who preceded him (e.g., Wyclif, Huss, and Savonarola), the Protestant Reformation Movement is generally dated from the time of Martin Luther. Luther, a Catholic monk, challenged the Roman Church (especially the papacy) when he nailed his ninety-five theses to the church door in Wittenberg, Germany on October 31, 1517. Luther, and others who came later (e.g., Calvin, Knox, Smyth), had no passionate desire to leave the church of their day; they merely wished to "reform" it of its abuses. As noble as their motives were, they succeeded only in creating many new denominations – bringing the "baggage" of Romanism with them as they formed movements. It would not be until a later time that men would have a clearer vision, abandoning the digressions of both Catholicism and Protestantism, with a call for the genuine "restoration" of primitive Christianity.

REGENERATION

The Greek term *palingenesia* consists of two components. *Palin* means "again, back," and *genesis,* denotes "to become, come about, birth." The word thus signifies a rebirth or a renewal. The actual word is found but twice in the N.T., though the idea is suggested frequently. (a) In Titus 3:5 the word refers to the process of conversion to Christ. Several points are made within this passage. Salvation is not accessed by works that men contrive; it is the result of God's mercy. Redemption is accomplished, however, by the *agency* of the "washing" of the rebirth, together with the renewing of the Holy Spirit. This process corresponds precisely with the Lord's instruction in John 3:3-5, namely the "born again" experience, which involves both the Holy Spirit and water. The Holy Spirit, working through the gospel message, produces the faith that expresses itself in the act of obeying Christ in baptism. See NEW BIRTH. Almost all scholars acknowledge that "washing" is a reference to water baptism. Note that the net result is being "justified by his grace" (v. 7). Obedience and grace are not mutually exclusive. (b) Near the close of his ministry, Jesus said unto his disciples: "Verily I say unto you, that you who have followed me, in the regeneration when the Son of man shall sit on the throne of his glory, you also shall sit upon twelve thrones, judging the twelve tribes of Israel" (Mt. 19:28). This passage has perplexed many. To what does "regeneration" refer in this text? It does not refer to a supposed "millennial reign" of Christ, nor to a "renewed earth," both theories being in contradiction to numerous scriptures – though it is difficult to find commentators who are not swayed by premillennial presupposition relative to this passage. See DISPENSATIONALISM. The passage most likely refers either to the authority of the apostles, as represented in the N.T. writings, in this *current age* of "regeneration," i.e., the Christian era, or else it envisions the apostles sharing in the *final victory* of their Lord (Rom. 8:17; 2 Tim. 2:12). Any view of this passage that one adopts must harmonize with the overall teaching of the Scriptures.

RELIGION

This term is found only a few times in the English Bible. In four cases it renders the Greek *threskeia*, which basically means holy service, the exercise of devotion to a transcendent Being or beings – whether true or false. In Acts 26:5 it is used of Judaism, yet in Colossians 2:18 it refers to the pagan worship of angels. *Threskeia* is twice used in James 1:26-27 with reference to the active benevolence expressed by those who

A Practical Handbook

espouse the teaching of Christ. In his presentation on Mars Hill, Paul referred to Greek heathenism as "religion" (*deisidaimonia*), literally a "reverence for demons," which is an allusion to false gods. In the modern world, "religion" has a much more elastic meaning. "Religion" can denote almost any philosophical viewpoint, e.g., Marxism, atheism, New Age pantheism, etc. Merely being "religious" is not enough to please God.

REPENTANCE

Repentance has a variety of uses in the Scriptures. (a) One form of "repentance" is simply a feeling of remorse. It was in this sense that Judas "repented" (Mt. 27:3) just before he hanged himself and perished eternally (Jn. 17:12). (b) Valid repentance is a "change of mind" that results in a change of conduct. That repentance is not simply "sorrow" alone, is evidenced by the fact that men, who were "pricked in their heart," nonetheless were instructed to "repent" (Acts 2:37-38). Paul states that "godly sorrow works [leads to] repentance" (2 Cor. 7:10). In both of these cases, the "repentance" obviously is something beyond mere emotional contrition. John the Baptist warned the rebellious Hebrews of his day that if they did not bring forth "fruit worthy of [corresponding to] repentance," they would be destroyed (Mt. 3:8-10). There can be no conversion to Christ where repentance is missing. One may be motivated to repentance by reflecting upon the goodness of God (Rom. 2:4), acknowledging the fact that the Creator has allowed us the opportunity to repent; such is a gracious extension of his benevolence (Acts 11:18). (c) When God is said to "repent" (cf. Gen. 6:6), the language is accommodative. This is a figure of speech called anthropopathism (man feelings), whereby human emotions are attributed to deity for the sake of emphasis. It is a way of stressing how displeased Heaven is with man's wickedness.

RESTORATION

The term "restoration" conveys a number of ideas in the Scriptures, depending upon the immediate context. (a) It may refer to the restitution of property or money in compliance to law (Dt. 22:2), or it may be a reflection of one's repentance (Lk. 19:8). (b) The term may be used of a spiritual invigoration (Psa. 23:3), or the return of one who has been overtaken in sin, to a right relationship with the Lord (Gal. 6:1). (c) Peter spoke of the fact that, following his ascension, Christ would remain in heaven "until the times of the restoration of all things" (Acts 3:21). What is the "restoration of all things" here in view? It is not universal salvation for mankind (Mt. 7:13-14), nor is it the "restoration of national Israel" in an earthly 1,000 year reign of Christ, as alleged by millennialists. This "restoration of all things" occurs *before* Christ returns from heaven (cf. Lk. 19:12, 15), not afterward. Peter identifies this "restoration" as "these days," i.e., the Christian age (Acts 3:24). The "restoration" contemplated in Acts 3:21, therefore, is the *implementation of God's gospel plan in the current dispensation*, whereby the lost can become "new creatures" again (2 Cor. 5:17). (d) In a more modern sense, the term "restoration" is used of the noble attempt of sincere people to return to the original pattern of Christianity, as revealed in the first century. It seeks to go back past Protestantism, back beyond the apostasy of Catholicism, and, with the New Testament as one's solitary guide, re-establish the teaching and practice of the original church. This is a glorious idea worthy of the attention of all serious Bible students.

RESURRECTION, CHRIST'S

The resurrection of Jesus Christ from the dead is the very foundation of Christianity. If the Lord was not raised, the religion of Christ is a hoax (cf. 1 Cor. 15:4; 14-19). The Savior's resurrection was foretold by the prophets (Psa. 16:8ff), and promised by Jesus himself (Jn. 2:19-22; Mt. 12:39-40; 16:21). On the third day following his death, Jesus was raised out of the grave, according to the unanimous testimony of the Gospel writers (Mt. 28:1ff; Mk. 16:1ff; Lk. 24:1ff; Jn. 20:1ff). From Pentecost onward, the early disciples unashamedly proclaimed the resurrection of their Lord (Acts 2:24, 32: 3:15, 26; 4:10, 33; 5:30; 10:40; 13:30, 33-34; 17:31). If Jesus was *not* raised from the dead, what happened to his body? There are but three possibilities: (a) The Lord's *enemies* took the body. But if that was the case, why did they not bring it forth, and thereby completely silence the preaching of the apostles? The answer is obvious. They did not have it. (b) The *disciples* recovered the body and kept it hid. This is not a credible explanation. These humble folks were willing to endure all manner of persecution – even violent death – rather than recant their testimony that they witnessed the Lord's presence following his death, or else they knew others who had seen the Savior (cf. 1 Cor. 15:1-11). While one may forfeit his life willingly for a "belief" he holds to be true, he will scarcely sacrifice himself for a proposition he *knows to be a lie*. Were James, Peter, and Paul all willing to die as martyrs, knowing very well that they lied about their knowledge of the resurrection of Jesus Christ? That is a theory too absurd for serious consideration. (c) The only option remaining is this: Jesus Christ was raised from the dead; Christianity is the true religion through which reconciliation with God may be enjoyed (Acts 4:11-12). Some scholars contend that a stone monument, believed to date from the time of Claudius

Caesar (cir. A.D. 40-50), reflects a Roman attempt to squelch the report that Jesus was raised from the dead. The inscription prohibits removing bodies from their tombs – under the penalty of death – and may constitute indirect evidence of the resurrection (Blaiklock).

RESURRECTION, GENERAL

The Bible clearly teaches that at the time of Christ's return, all the dead will be raised from their interment. (a) In the Patriarchal age, Job seems to allude to the hope of the resurrection (Job. 19:25-26). Abraham believed that God was able to raise Isaac from the dead (Heb. 11:19). (b) Moses, speaking on behalf of God, declared: "I kill, and I make alive" (Dt. 32:39). Daniel prophesied that the dead of the earth would awake, some to life everlasting, some to eternal shame and contempt (Dan. 12:2). (c) During his ministry, Jesus promised there would be a future resurrection of both the good and the evil (Jn. 5:28-29). When the Sadducees, who disbelieved in the resurrection (Mt. 22:23), attempted to dispute with Christ regarding this doctrine, the Savior informed them that their dogma reflected ignorance of the Scriptures and the power of God (Mt. 22:29). (d) The apostles of Christ vigorously argued for the doctrine of the bodily resurrection (see Acts 24:15). The entire 15th chapter of 1 Corinthians deals with this theme. There Paul contends for the following. Christ was raised from the dead (1-11). His resurrection is the guarantee of that resurrection to come (12-24). The dead will come forth from the grave – not in a physical form, but in a spiritual body (35-49). The bodily resurrection is a token of the ultimate victory of Christ's cause (50-58). In the final book of the N.T., Jesus contends that he has the "keys" of death and Hades (Rev. 1:18), which implies the resurrection of the body from the state of death, and the deliverance of the soul from the hadean realm.

RETRIBUTION

Retribution will be the dispensing of the "wrath of God," as an expression of divine justice, upon those who have persisted in wicked rebellion against their Maker. The expression "wrath of God" is found about twelve times in the English Bible. One term in the Greek N.T., that suggests the divine disposition for retribution is *thumos*, anger that "boils," while another word is *orge*, which hints of an abiding and settled state of mind (Trench). Perhaps these two terms in concert depict the *intensity* of God's righteous judgment, and the *sustained determination* to punish the incorrigible. Here are some facts regarding Heaven's retribution. (a) It is not impulsive; rather, it is characterized by great patience (Gen. 6:3; Ex. 34:6). (b) When evil men persistently reject the Lord, he is willing "to show his wrath and make his power known" (Rom. 9:22). The great Flood of Noah's day is evidence aplenty of this. (c) The final exhibition of his retribution will be thorough and abiding (Mt. 3:12; Rom. 1:18). (d) Retribution will be just; it will be a day of the revelation of the *righteous* judgment of God (Gen. 18:25; Rom. 2:5; cf. Rev. 19:11) upon those who have earned their just reward (Rom. 6:23). These are "vessels" who have "fitted themselves" for destruction (Rom. 9:22; see "destruction" in Vine). (d) Retribution is not arbitrary (as Calvinism alleges); rather, any man may escape it, for God is not willing that anyone should perish (2 Pet. 3:9). Those who obey the gospel can be "saved from the wrath of God" (Rom. 5:9).

RETURN OF CHRIST

During his earthly ministry, Jesus promised that, following his death and ascension back to heaven, he would "come again" eventually (Jn. 14:3; cf. Mt. 24:37ff; 25:31ff). When he left the earth, angels vowed he would return again (Acts 1:10-11). The doctrine of the second coming was steadfastly proclaimed by the writers of the N.T. (a) The return of Christ is *certain*, being buttressed by the fact that the Lord was raised from the dead (Acts 17:31). (b) Christ's return will be *uncertain* in terms of the time. It will be an unexpected event (Mt. 24:37ff). The date-setters have all been wrong. (c) Christ's coming will be *visible* (2 Thes. 1:7; Heb. 9:28) and *audible* (1 Thes. 4:16; 2 Pet. 3:10) – not secretly and silently, as in the "Rapture" theory. See RAPTURE. (d) At his coming, the Savior will *raise all the dead* (Jn. 5:28-29; Acts 24:15; 1 Cor. 15:23). (e) The great Judgment Day will occur at the time of the Savior's return (Mt. 25: 31ff; Acts 17:31; 2 Cor. 5:10), at which point the righteous and wicked will be separated (Mt. 13:30, 48). (f) Those who have been obedient to the Lord will inherit eternal life, and those who have refused him will suffer everlasting punishment (Dan. 12:2; Mt. 25:46; 13:41-43). (g) Consummating Christ's return will be the destruction of the material Universe. As God spoke it into existence, so, by his word, it will be destroyed (Mt. 24:35; 2 Pet. 3:1-13).

REVELATION, BOOK OF

This final book of the N.T. is a fitting conclusion to the sacred canon. Written by John, while exiled on the island of Patmos, it is directed primarily to seven congregations in Asia Minor; the principles are obviously applicable to all Christians. The book was written in a time of great danger for the followers of

Christ, hence, its message is largely in symbols borrowed from the O.T. This "smuggles" a word of hope to the persecuted, without compounding their danger. The message is one of victory; the Lamb will overcome his enemies (e.g., the dragon, the beast, and the false prophet), and those who follow him will share in the victory on the day of Judgment (cf. 19:11-16).

REVELATION OF GOD

The revelation of God has to do with the processes by which the Creator has made himself known to his rational creation. (a) Jehovah has revealed himself to humanity in the abstract features of the Cosmos (that which has order) – the Universe. The heavens declare his glory (Psa. 19:1), and his invisible qualities (power, wisdom, etc.) are seen in the things that are made (Rom. 1:20). (b) God has revealed himself in the operational procedures of his providential activity. His use of dignitaries like Cyrus of Persia (Isa. 44:28; 45:1ff) defy human explanation. (c) The Lord has shown himself in the sensitivity of the human conscience; even men who have no written revelation from Heaven possess an awareness that "right" and "wrong" exist (Rom. 2:14-15) – though they may be unable to define precisely how these are to be measured. (d) God has revealed himself in a tangible form, by the incarnate presence of his Son upon the earth twenty centuries ago (Jn. 1:18; 14:9). (e) Our Maker has revealed himself finally in a series of sixty-six, inerrant documents, the authenticity of which is attested by a variety of amazing evidences. Truly, "God has spoken" (Heb. 1:1). See BIBLE.

RIGHTEOUS

Righteous is the state or quality of being right. (a) Only Deity is righteous in the *absolute* sense (Rom. 3:10). To speak of the righteousness of God is to affirm his absolute morality, and the expectation he entertains for purity in those fashioned in his image (Gen. 17:1; 1 Pet. 1:15). God will judge consistent with his own character (Psa. 9:4), and he will always do that which is right (Gen. 18:25). When one is inclined to wonder how the Creator will fairly judge humanity, this concept must be borne in mind. On the final day of history, the revelation of the "righteous judgment of God" will shine in such brilliance that every knee will bow and every tongue will confess his glory (Rom. 2:5; 14:11). (b) Jehovah's righteousness is set forth in the gospel (Rom. 1:16-17). When one submits to the requirements of the gospel (Rom. 6:17), the atoning effect of Christ's death cancels all his past sins and Heaven accounts to him the status of being "righteous" (Rom. 3:21ff; Phil. 3:9). (c) The Christian will never reach a state of absolute righteousness as long as he abides in the flesh (Rom. 7:14ff; Phil. 3:12-13), but, in a *relative* sense, he is viewed as righteous (cf. Jas. 5:16).

ROMANS, BOOK OF

Paul's letter to the Christians in Rome develops the theme of God's gospel plan of justification for sinful man on the ground Christ's atoning death. The book demonstrates that redemption could not be effected by means of the law of Moses; rather, it is achieved through "the faith" system. While salvation is received on the basis of "faith," it is not an inactive faith, but an obedient faith (1:5; 16:26). The sinner receives "newness of life" when he is buried with Christ in baptism (6:3ff).

RUTH, BOOK OF

The book of Ruth has to do with a godly Moabite woman, Ruth by name, who joined herself to the Hebrew people during the days of the judges. She was a widow who married an Israelite by the name of Boaz. She became the great-grandmother of David, hence, was an ancestress of Jesus Christ. As a Gentile, she represents a preview of the international nature of the Lord's kingdom. The book covers a span of about ten years during the early era of the judges.

SABBATH

The term "sabbath" is derived from the Hebrew *shabath*, to "cease." The use of this word for the "seventh day" reflects the Genesis account of creation, when, after six days of creative activity, Jehovah "ceased" his labor (cf. Ex. 20:8-11). There is no astronomical phenomenon to explain a seven-day week, as there is for the month or the year. Only the creation record provides an historical rationale for the week. Some facts regarding the term "sabbath" are as follows. (a) "Sabbath" is a generic word; it may refer to the seventh day (Ex. 20:8ff), to certain other sacred celebrations, e.g., the day of Atonement (Lev. 16:31; 23:32), or to a year during which the land was to be allowed its rest (Lev. 25:2ff; cf. 2 Chron. 36:21). (b) The seventh-day sabbath was not a moral regulation for the whole of humanity from the commencement of the creation. Rather, it was given as a "sign" between Jehovah and Israel (Dt. 5:1ff; Ezek. 20:12), at Sinai (Neh. 9:13-14) – though there was a preliminary trial sabbath just prior to that event (Ex. 16:4ff). Genesis 2:3, written by Moses many centuries after the creation week, merely states the purpose of the sabbath's sanctification, not the time of that event. (c) The purpose of the sabbath was to commemorate the creation activity, provide rest for man and beast, and to pre-figure the ultimate "rest" of heaven (Ex. 20:8ff; Heb. 4:9; Rev. 14:13). (d) The law of Moses – with its various ordinances (including the sabbath) – was abolished by Christ (Eph. 2:14ff; Col. 2:14), so that under the Christian age, one is not to be "judged" [condemned] for failing to observe the sabbath (Col. 2:16). (e) Sunday is a day of worship for Christians (Acts 20:7; 1 Cor. 16:2), but it is not to be designated as the "Christian sabbath."

SAINT

This word is derived from a Greek term meaning "separated." (a) "Saint" refers to an ordinary member of Christ's church who has submitted to gospel obedience (Phil. 1:1; 4:21; 2 Thes. 1:10). (b) A saint (*hagios*) is one who has gone through the process of sanctification (*hagiasmos*). See SANCTIFIED. It thus denotes one who has been "separated" from the world, and who enjoys a special relationship with Christ. (c) The process involved in becoming a "saint" includes: believing in the Lord (Mk. 16:16), repenting of sin (Acts 2:38), and consummating these acts of obedience by the "washing of water" (Eph. 5:26; 1 Cor. 6:11) – an allusion to baptism. Note the use of "sanctified" in these passages. (d) The dogma of "sainthood" – arrived at by "beautification" and "canonization" – (as in the Roman Catholic system) is completely alien to the New Testament.

SALVATION

"Salvation" is the result of having been "saved." The verb "save" (*sozo*) had a variety of ancient meanings. It could signify to deliver, to heal, to liberate, to preserve, etc., depending upon the context. Most prominently in the N.T. it has to do with deliverance from the guilt and ultimate consequence (spiritual death) of sin. Some "salvation" facts are: (a) Ultimately, salvation is from God; no sinful creature has the ability to save himself (Eph. 2:8-9; Tit. 3:4-5). (b) Salvation was made possible through the redemptive mission of Jesus of Nazareth (Mt. 1:21; Lk. 2:9-11; Acts 4:12; Rom. 3:21ff). (c) The plan of salvation is revealed in the gospel message (Rom. 1:16-17; Eph. 1:13). (d) Human beings have a role to play in salvation; they are not merely passive objects in the process (Acts 2:40; Phil. 2:12; 1 Pet. 4:17-18). (e) There is an immediate salvation at the point of baptism (Mk. 16:16), but there is also a salvation at the end of life (Rom. 13:11; 1 Pet. 1:5, 9), provided one has remained faithful to his Lord. (f) It is possible to "neglect" one's salvation and finally be lost (Heb. 2:3; Acts 8:13, 20).

SAMUEL 1, BOOK OF

This book contains the historical record of the change in Israel's form of government from judges to that of the kings. The nation, in an act of rejecting God, desired a king to be like their pagan neighbors (1 Sam. 8:4ff). The book spans more than a century, from the birth of Samuel to the death of Israel's first king, Saul. This document is also important in that it gives considerable material relative to the rise of Israel's greatest king, David (1 Sam. 16ff). In the Hebrew Bible, 1 and 2 Samuel constitute a single book.

SAMUEL 2, BOOK OF

This book contains the record of the forty-year administration of the Hebrews' most illustrious ruler, David, who was an ancestor of the Lord Jesus Christ. The book details David's victories, his weaknesses, and his contrite disposition. His administration was racked with controversy and rebellion, but overall David was an effective ruler. One of his nobler achievements was in preparing the material that eventually would go into the construction of God's temple.

SANCTIFIED

Sanctified suggests "having been separated from (something), set apart." The term is used in a variety of ways in the Bible. (a) Both God the Father and Christ the Son are to be sanctified (Num. 20:12; 27:14; 1 Pet. 3:15), which means they are to be set apart as unique and authoritative Sovereigns over our lives. (b) God sanctifies (sets apart as holy) those who respond to his truth (Jn. 17:17) in obedience to the gospel (Eph. 5:26; 1 Cor. 6:11). (c) Man sanctifies himself by exercising his power of choice and yielding to the will of God (Lev. 11:44; 1 Pet. 1:15). (d) The basis of spiritual sanctification is the death of Christ (Heb. 9:13-14; 10:10). (e) Occasionally "sanctified" takes on a special sense. For example, the unbeliever who is married to a Christian is sanctified by the believer (1 Cor. 7:14). This does not mean that the marriage itself *saves* the non-Christian. Rather, the sense seems to be that the unbeliever, being in close proximity with the Christian spouse, is in a kind of "set apart" environment – cut off from the extreme godless influence of the world. The end result is the happy possibility that the sinner may be won to the Lord through Christian influence. Again, elsewhere Paul speaks of the fact that "every creature of God" (i.e., every kind of meat) has been sanctified (1 Tim. 4:4-5). Under the O.T. regime, certain creatures were forbidden as food (see Lev. 11). Under Christian law, all meats are acceptable for food. They have been authorized for human consumption by the "word of God," and, by our prayers of thanksgiving, they are set apart for our good use. See also SAINT, HOLY.

SATAN

The Hebrew term *satan* ("adversary" - one who "cherishes animosity") comes over into Greek as *diabolos* ("slanderer, accuser"). Satan is a spirit-being who is the arch-enemy of God and man. His characteristic activity is to "tempt" (Mt. 4:3), and his destiny is eternal torment (Rev. 20:10). See DEVIL.

SCRIPTURE

The Greek term *graphe* ("writing") comes into the English Bible (via Latin, *scriptura*) as "scripture." The word almost always has the definite article "the scriptures." The expression may refer to a *particular* passage, e.g., "have you not read this scripture?" (Mk. 12:10 - citing Psa. 118:22), or it may denote the *whole* of the O.T. canon (Jn. 5:39). Usually "scriptures" will refer to the O.T., but the word may embrace the N.T. writings as well. Peter, by implication, referred to Paul's "epistles" as scripture (see 2 Pet. 3:16, "other scriptures"). A consideration of the use of "scriptures" in the Bible reveals several things. (a) The term "scripture" or "scriptures" takes on a technical sense, having to do with a document of *divine origin* (2 Tim. 3:16-17). (b) The "scriptures" speak as the *authoritative* voice of God (Rom. 9:17; Gal. 3:8). (c) One must not venture into the territory beyond that which is authorized by "the things which are written" (1 Cor. 4:6 ASV; cf. 2 Jn. 9). See BIBLE.

Bible Words and Theological Terms Made Easy

SEPTUAGINT

The Septuagint is a Greek translation of the Hebrew Old Testament. It dates from the third century before Christ. The "Letter of Aristeas" (cir. 100 B.C.) suggests that this version was translated in Egypt for the purpose of providing Greek-speaking Jews with access to the Hebrew Scriptures. Tradition (questionable) has it that the Septuagint was translated by seventy-two men. The version thus is commonly referred to as the LXX (rounded-off Roman numeral for the seventy-two). Some sections adhere closely to the Hebrew text; other areas are considerably "looser." Nonetheless, because this was the common Bible of the Greek-speaking world in the first century, Jesus and the N.T. writers frequently quoted from this version. See also VERSIONS.

SEVENTY WEEKS

Near the end of that historical period known as the Babylonian captivity, the prophet Daniel received a marvelous revelation that involved the unveiling of future events relative to the coming of Christ. The narrative is recorded in Daniel 9:24-27. The prophecy may be studied from three viewpoints. (a) It describes certain things to be *accomplished* by the coming of the "anointed one," (the Messiah). The Christ will: finish transgression, make an end of sins, and effect reconciliation for iniquity. Further, he will usher in a plan for everlasting righteousness, he will seal up vision and prophecy, terminate animal sacrifices, and make firm a new covenant. These descriptives detail the *redemptive* mission of Jesus. (b) A specific *chronology* is set forth, under the symbolism of "seventy weeks," literally, 490 years. The starting point is with the "command to restore and rebuild Jerusalem" (457 B.C.), and the

A Practical Handbook

terminal point is that time when the "anointed one" is "cut off," (i.e., the death of Christ - A.D. 30). Ancient Jerusalem would be rebuilt within the first "week" (49 years). The second division (434 years) would end with the commencement of Jesus' ministry. In the "midst" of the final week (after a ministry of three and one-half years), the Messiah would be "cut off" (die). (c) Finally, the *consequences* of the Jews rejection of their Messiah are detailed. The Roman "prince" (Titus) would come and assault Jerusalem. The city would be *desolated* by this *abominable* force, and the Jewish temple would be destroyed. Jesus referred to this prophecy in his Olivet discourse (see Mt. 24:15). See ABOMINATION OF DESOLATION.

SIN

More than a dozen words are used in the Greek N.T. to represent various aspects of "sin" (e.g., bad, evil, transgression, iniquity, trespass, godless, unrighteous, etc.). The most frequently employed word is *hamartia* (173 times), which provides the picture of "missing the mark." The word is used literally in the Greek version of the O.T. for soldiers who could hurl stones with the sling and not *miss* (Jdg. 20:16). Sin is the transgression of God's law, whether by overt commission (1 Jn. 3:4), or by omission (Jas. 4:17). (a) Sin originated with the rebellion of Satan (1 Jn. 3:8), and the angels who followed him (2 Pet. 2:4; cf. Jude 6). (b) While Satan certainly tempts humans to sin (Mt. 4:3), man yields by his own choice (Jas. 1:13-14), for this enemy can be resisted (Jas. 4:7). (c) Sin is universal, afflicting all who have reached an age of moral and spiritual responsibility (Gen. 8:21; Rom. 3:10, 23). See ORIGINAL SIN. (d) Sin has affected man's environment (Gen. 3:18; 8:11; see FLOOD), his health (Gen. 2:17; Rom. 5:12), and his relationship with God (Isa. 56:1-2; Eph. 2:1ff). (e) Jesus Christ came to earth and was subjected to temptation, but he never sinned (Heb. 4:15; 1 Pet. 2:21). He was qualified, therefore, to die for man's sin (Isa. 53:4-6; Mt. 26:28; 1 Cor. 15:3). (f) Forgiveness of sin is possible for those who surrender in faith to God and to his Son (Heb. 11:6; Jn. 8:24). One must change his life from wrong to right through repentance (Lk. 13:3, 5; Acts 2:38; 17:30-31). Union with Christ is effected finally by being buried in the water of baptism (Mk. 16:16; Acts 2:38; 22:16; 1 Pet. 3:21). For the Christian who sins, forgiveness is obtained through repentance and prayer (Acts 8:22).

SLAVERY

The term "slave" (Grk. *doulos*) is used in the Bible in both a literal and a figurative sense. (a) *Literal* slaves were common in the ancient world. A person could be purchased as a slave, become a slave as spoil of war, be born into a slave family, or sell himself into slavery. In most countries the slave had no rights – he was not a person but a piece of property to be treated harshly and disposed of by the will of his master. While the Hebrews owned slaves, the O.T. law was far superior to that of the pagan nations in regulating the institution. Slaves were to be treated kindly (cf. Ex. 21:2-27; Lev. 25:25-55). A slave who ran away from his master could not be forcibly brought back (Dt. 23:15). In the first century, some Christians owned slaves (Eph. 6:5, 9; Philm. 10-16). It was not the design of the Christian system to create a revolution by advocating the violent overthrow of this institution – which quite obviously was never the divine ideal. Rather, the N.T. contains the "seeds" of benevolence (cf. Mt. 7:12) that eventually abolishes this practice in most civilized nations (cf. Gal. 3:28; Eph. 6:5-9; Philm.).

(b) The "slave" concept is used *symbolically* is several ways. The person who keeps on practicing sin, in an unrestrained fashion, becomes a "slave" to evil (Jn. 8:34; Rom. 6:17). There is a sense in which Jesus assumed the role of a slave in going to the cross for us (Phil. 2:7ff). When the Christian surrenders all his personal interests, yielding himself wholly to the will of God, he becomes a slave of his Lord, Jesus Christ (Rom. 1:1; Phil. 1:1); only then is he truly free.

SON OF GOD

Before Jesus was born, the angel informed Mary: "...the holy thing which is begotten shall be called the Son of God" (Lk. 1:35). The descriptive reveals something of the unique essence of Christ. The phrase "son of" is sometimes employed in the Scriptures to depict the *nature* of someone (cf. Mk. 3:17; Jn. 17:12). The Gospel accounts refer to Jesus as being the Son of God some 150 times. (a) He is described as the "Son" in O.T. prophecy (Psa. 2:7; Hos. 11:1). (b) God himself acknowledged Jesus as his Son (Mt. 3:17; 17:5). (c) Based upon undeniable evidence, the disciples recognized Christ as God's Son (Mt. 16:16). (d) Some of the Lord's enemies even conceded his divine Sonship (Mt. 27:54). (e) Jesus made a clear distinction between the nature of *his* relationship to the Father, and that which others enjoy in an accommodative fashion. In his prayers he never prayed "our" Father; rather, it was "my" Father (Mt. 11:25; Mk. 14:36; Jn. 11:41; cf. Jn. 20:17). Jesus claimed that God was *his own* Father in a unique sense (Jn. 5:18). The person who refuses to believe that Jesus is the Son of God cannot possibly be right with the Heavenly Father (see Lk. 10:16).

SON OF MAN

The expression "Son of Man" is found mostly in the Gospel accounts (some 80 times) – especially the Synoptics (see) – and it is the term Christ used more than any other to designate himself. In fact, only he uses it of himself. The word is a Messianic title with roots in the O.T. (cf. Dan. 7:13). One aspect of the phrase is to identify Jesus as an actual *human* being. On the other hand, the expression is also employed to stress the Lord's authority as a divine being. It is as "Son of man" that he will exercise divine judgment (Jn. 5:27). Note how the phrases "Son of man" and "Son of God" are used interchangeably in Matthew 16:13-16. "Son of man" is used in relation to Jesus' atoning death in Mark 10:45.

SONG OF SOLOMON, BOOK OF

This small book contains one of the 1,005 songs penned by king Solomon (1 Kgs. 4:32). It extols the passion and bliss of wedded love, and praises the king's "beloved." Many scholars have suggested that the theme is illustrative of God's love for Israel, and Christ's love for his church. It is a tragedy that Solomon's passion for *many* women led him into deep apostasy (cf. 1 Kgs. 11:3-4), which perhaps he regretted in his advanced years. Ecclesiastes may reflect a wiser disposition.

SOUL, SPIRIT

The word "soul" is used in several senses in the Bible. (a) It may signify an individual person (Ezek. 18:20). (b) It may be employed of mere biological life (Gen. 1:30). (c) It can have to do with that eternal aspect of man that is in the very image of God (Mt. 10:28). "Spirit" may be used in different senses as well. (a) It can depict the nature of a non-material being, e.g. God (Jn. 4:24; Lk. 24:39; cf. "Holy Spirit"), or angels (Heb. 1:14). (b) "Spirit" can be used, by way of the figure known as synecdoche (part for the whole), for a person (1 Jn. 4:1). (c) Spirit may refer the "inner man" that is fashioned in God's image (1 Cor. 5:5; 16:18; 2 Cor. 7:1; Jas. 2:26). (d) Spirit can stand for a disposition, e.g., spirit of fear, etc. (2 Tim. 1:7), or a meek and submissive spirit (cf. 1 Pet. 3:4). See MAN.

SOVEREIGNTY OF GOD

The term "sovereign" denotes the *right* that God has to rule the Universe. (Note that the word "reign" is contained within "sovereign.") Jehovah has this "right" because he is the *Creator*, and therefore the Owner, of every thing that has been made (Psa. 24:1; Mt. 20:15). Does not the potter have a "right" over the clay (see Rom. 9:20-21; cf. Eph. 1:11)? It is the epitome of arrogance to suggest otherwise (cf. Isa. 29:16). If one expects to enjoy heaven, he must yield to the sovereign will of God as made known through the sacred Scriptures (see 1 Chron. 29:11; Ezek. 18:4; Dan. 4:35).

SPIRITUAL

The adjective "spiritual" has several senses. (a) It may refer to a being that is "spirit" in nature, e.g., angels (Eph. 6:12). (b) Spiritual may denote that which is from God, thus is lofty in its quality (Rom. 7:14). (c) Spiritual may connote a person who has access to sacred revelation by supernatural means of the Spirit's operation (1 Cor. 2:6ff). (d) The term may be set in contrast to the secular, as in "spiritual songs" (Eph. 5:19). (e) Spiritual may describe one who is knowledgeable and strong

Bible Words and Theological Terms Made Easy

in the faith, as opposed to the uninformed, weak person (1 Cor. 3:1; Gal. 6:1). Those who would possess the character of the "spiritual" (cf. Gal. 6:1), must be "led by the Spirit" and "walk by the Spirit," as the Spirit instructs via the written word (Eph. 6:17). Thereby one is able to cultivate the "fruit of the Spirit" (Gal. 5:16, 18, 22-23).

SUFFERING

"Suffering" is a term that embraces the various physical and emotional ills to which the human family is heir. Skeptics charge that human suffering is irreconcilable with the idea of an all-powerful, benevolent God. If God were able, and willing, to remedy man's misfortunes, it is alleged, he would. Since he has not, that must suggest there is no powerful and gracious God overseeing human affairs. The argument is false for it fails to take into consideration the fact that a good and powerful God may *allow* suffering for a *noble end* that man cannot see at present. Here are some points to ponder. (a) The Creator is not directly responsible for man's ailments; his creation, as it issued from him initially, was "very good" (Gen. 1:31). It is obvious, therefore, that suffering is a subsequent development. (b) Suffering is a necessary by-product of man being given the ability to make free choices. If human beings have the ability to make choices, there must be negative consequences attached to evil choices – otherwise, there would never be the inclination to choose good over bad. (c) We suffer negative consequences for personal decisions we make (1 Pet. 4:15), and we suffer the consequences of bad choices others have made – both in the past and in the present (Ex. 20:4-6; Rom. 5:12; see FLOOD). (d) Suffering helps to build character, producing the best traits of which men are capable (Rom. 5:3; Jas. 1:3; 1 Pet.

1:7). (e) Without the possibility of suffering, there would have been no plan of redemption for fallen humanity (Heb. 5:8-9; 12:1ff). (f) The book of Job reveals that suffering may have a goal of which man is not aware. Even in hardship, then, one must learn to trust God and be obedient to his will (Job 13:15; Eccl. 12:12-13).

SYNOPTICS

The term "synoptic" derives from the Greek word *sunoptikos,* which means "seeing the whole together." The word is used to describe the first three Gospel narratives – Matthew, Mark, and Luke – because these records are viewed as portraying the life of Jesus from a rather common vantagepoint. (John's Gospel account is more topically structured and universally directed.) The "synoptic" theme also deals with the relationship of the documents to one another and their different points of emphasis. For example, Matthew writes principally for the Jews. He frequently quotes the O.T. Scriptures, and he emphasizes the kingly authority of Christ. Mark writes for the Romans. He stresses the deeds of Christ and focuses upon the Lord as the ideal servant who carries out the Father's will with urgency. Luke directs his message to the Greeks and his emphasis is upon the manhood of Jesus; he also heralds the international thrust of the gospel. While there are comparative differences in the synoptic accounts (each containing some material peculiar to it), they do not contradict one another. The records supplement each other, and the differences reveal a lack of collusion. The early church considered all three narratives to be inspired of God and authoritative as historical records.

TABERNACLE

The Greek word *skene* (rendered "tabernacle") means a "tent." (a) The tabernacle of Moses' day was a tent of worship, designed by God, and provided for the children of Israel as they wandered in the wilderness of Sinai. It was the appointed place where Jehovah would "meet" with his people (Ex. 25-28; 35-40). The tabernacle was a prototype of the temple, which would be built in the time of Solomon. (b) The tabernacle/temple arrangement was a "type" (pictorial, prophetic preview) of things to come later. The "holy place" within the tabernacle prefigured the church (cf. Heb. 9:1-10), and the "holy of holies" foreshadowed heaven (Heb. 9:11ff). Under the new covenant regime, the temple of God is the body of Christ (1 Cor. 3:16; Eph. 2:19-22; 1 Pet. 2:5). The prophecy of Amos 9:11-12, regarding the rebuilding of the "tabernacle of David," is fulfilled in the church (Acts 15:14ff), and not in an alleged "millennial reign" of Christ upon the earth. (c) The incarnation of Christ, i.e., deity dwelling in a human body, is referred to as a tabernacle dwelling (cf. "dwelt," *skenoo*, in John 1:14). (d) Our current physical body is called "the earthly house of our tabernacle" (2 Cor. 5:1; cf. v. 4). This implies two things: there is an entity, the "spirit," that lives within our "tabernacle" (Jas. 2:26); and, this physical dwelling place is temporary, to be replaced by a permanent, immortal dwelling (1 Cor. 15).

TALMUD

The Talmud is an encyclopedia of Jewish cultural tradition that was designed to supplement the Hebrew Old Testament. It evolved over an era from about 450 B.C. to A.D. 500. The Talmud (from a Hebrew word which means "study") developed in two stages. The oldest was the Mishnah ("to repeat"),

A Practical Handbook

a section of six main segments which dealt with agricultural laws, festivals, family matters, civil/criminal laws, temple laws, impurities, etc. Later came the Gemara ("learning"), which contained the discussions of the Jewish rabbis relative to the Mishnah. The Mishnah, usually referred to as the "oral law," was in existence in a written form by the end of the second century A.D.; the Gemara, the commentary on the law, was formed between A.D. 200-500. When Jesus referred to the "traditions" of the fathers (Mt. 15:1ff; Mk. 7:3ff), he was speaking of those human rules (frequently bound by the rabbis as "law") which were later incorporated into the written Talmud. The Talmud provides scholars with a rich depository of information about Jewish beliefs and practices in the first century.

TEACH, TEACHER

The role of the Christian teacher is sobering indeed, for those who presume to "teach" will receive a "heavier judgment" (Jas. 3:1). This warning is not designed to discourage teaching (a divine obligation – Mt. 28:20); rather, it emphasizes that the responsibility must be taken very seriously. (a) The gospel teacher must be *faithful* in his Christian life. Paul urged Timothy to commit the truth to "faithful men [people], who shall be able to teach others" (2 Tim. 2:2). (b) The teacher must be *zealous in his preparation*, for there is no inspired person today who receives his message supernaturally, "in that hour," as he speaks (Mt. 10:19). The teacher, therefore, must be "diligent" ("study" KJV) to show himself as an "approved" spokesman for God. The verb *spoudazo* ("give diligence" ASV) signifies exertion, zealousness, earnestness, etc. (c) The Christian teacher must *speak the truth*, for only truth can set a man free (Jn. 8:32). (d) He will also speak that truth *lovingly* (Eph. 4:

15); teaching is not an exercise in seeking personal victory, but to win souls. (e) The godly teacher will not grow weary but will teach *persistently*, "in season and out of season" (2 Tim. 4:1ff). Remember, Jesus was *supremely* a Teacher (Jn. 3:1), and if one would be like him, he must recognize his responsibility to teach.

TEMPTATION

The original words that are rendered by the English "tempt" are employed in two broad senses in the Scriptures, depending upon the context in which they are found. First, the concept may be that of putting something to the "test" to determine its character. David did not want to use Saul's armor because it had not been "proved" (1 Sam. 17:39). Second, the sense can be quite sinister – that of a "solicitation to evil." Several examples prove helpful in understanding this subject. (a) God put Abraham to the test when he commanded him to offer Isaac (Gen. 22:1; cf. Ex. 16:4; Jdg. 2:22). Examples of how men pass the testing process provide encouragement to others – to persevere in their faith (cf. Heb. 11:17ff). (b) "Tempt" is used in a negative way to illustrate how men exhibit weak faith in putting God on "trial," i.e., they defiantly challenge him (Ex. 17:2; Psa. 78:18ff; Mt. 4:7; Acts 5:9). (c) Satan tempts (entices) people to sin by the use of certain methods allowed by God in the providential scheme of things upon earth (Job 1:12; 2:6; 1 Cor. 10:13; 1 Pet. 5:8; Rev. 12). Good people fight against such temptations (Jas. 4:7), and seek to serve God with faithfulness. (d) The devil sought to seduce Christ through the three major avenues of temptation – desire of the flesh, the lust of the eyes, and the vainglory of life (1 Jn. 2:15) – but the Lord resisted all such assaults (Heb. 4:15), by appealing to the Scriptures (Mt.

4:1-11). (e) People can arm themselves against temptation by incorporating God's words into their hearts (Psa. 119:11), and through prayer (Mt. 6:13; 26:41).

TEN COMMANDMENTS

The "Ten Commandments" constituted the core element of the law of Moses (see Ex. 19:16-20:17). They were written by God himself on the two tables of stone (Ex. 31:18; 32:15-16; 34:1, 28; Dt. 10:4). Moses shattered the first set when he learned of Israel's worship of the golden calf (Ex. 32:19). Eventually, the second set was deposited in the ark of the covenant, which was kept in the tabernacle's holy of holies (Ex. 25:16; 40:20). (a) The commands fall into two categories – religious and moral laws. The first four set forth certain obligations the Jews had to God; the final six regulate the conduct of the Hebrew people among themselves. (b) The commandments embody certain principles that were right or wrong from the beginning of time. For example, it was wrong for Cain to murder Abel long before the prohibition was formalized in the Law. The Sabbath law, however, appears to have been unique to Israel. See SABBATH. (c) The Ten Commandments, as a legal system, were abolished at the cross (Rom. 7:4, 6-7; 2 Cor. 3:1ff; Eph. 2:14-15; Col. 2:14-17). Some of the same legal *principles* are a part of the new covenant, which was foreshadowed by the old, but the Mosaic code, as such, is gone. (d) In the Sermon on the Mount, Jesus emphasized that the moral requirements of *his* law go much deeper than the rather external approach of Moses' law (cf. Mt. 5:21, 27). (e) There are several modern perversions of the Ten Commandments. Catholic theologians frequently "abridge" the first portion (eliminating the second commandment – the prohibition regarding the worship of *images*), and divide the tenth commandment into two, so as to retain the full complement of *ten*. Some cults, e.g., the Seventh-day Adventists, attempt to bind the sabbath day in the Christian age, though they inconsistently ignore the death penalty requirement that was associated with it under the Mosaic regime. Millennialists allege that the Mosaic law, with the Commandments, will be revived in that mythical thousand-year reign from Jerusalem. See DISPENSATIONALISM.

TEXT OF THE BIBLE

The Old Testament was originally written in Hebrew (with certain minor portions in Aramaic), while the New Testament was penned in *Koine* Greek. None of the original documents (called autographs) of either Testament is extant today – and for good reason. Likely men would worship them as idols if they were accessible. What scholars have done, therefore, is to gather the available ancient evidence, and from this evidence construct a Hebrew text and a Greek text from which modern translations derive. (a) There are tens of thousands of manuscripts (whole or fragments) of the Hebrew O.T. Some of the most valuable are the Dead Sea Scrolls, representing parts of all O.T. books except Esther. The discovery of those texts in 1947 pushed our knowledge of the O.T. back about 1,000 years earlier than the evidence previously possessed. This fabulous find demonstrated the amazing accuracy of the scribal copying process of the O.T. manuscripts across the centuries. By a comparison of the available data, noted scholar Robert D. Wilson confidently argued, on the basis of ancient manuscripts, versions, and secular inscriptions, that one may be "scientifically certain" that the modern text of the O.T. is "substantially the same text" as that "written by the original composers of the Old Testament documents." (b) The restoration of the Greek text of the N.T. is even more impressive. The evidence consists of three main categories. There are more than 5,300 Greek manuscripts, some fragments of which extend back to the second century A.D. This body of evidence is much more substantial than what exists for the Greek classics. There are literally thousands of ancient versions (translations of the N.T. into languages other than Greek), and some of these are quite early. This is remarkable since the ancients rarely translated documents from one tongue to another. Too, there are thousands of quotations from the N.T. in the writings of the early "church fathers" (of the first two centuries of Christian history). Virtually all of the N.T. could be reproduced from these documents alone. From these various sources, the science of "textual criticism" has constructed Greek texts upon which our present translations are based. All of this evidence provides a solid foundation for confidence in the integrity of the English Bible. See also TRANSLATION.

THESSALONIANS 1, BOOK OF

The church in Thessalonica was established on Paul's second missionary journey (Acts 17:1ff). After he left the region, he received a report regarding the congregation in Thessalonica, containing both positive and negative news. This letter, written from Corinth (Acts 18:1, 5), is a response to that report. The epistle commends the brethren for their faith and love (3:6). However, Paul is also forced to defend himself against the accusations of certain critics (2:3-6, 17-18). Too, there was confusion regarding the matter of Christ's second coming (1:10; 2:12, 19; 3:13; 4:11-18; 5:1-11, 23). There are also exhortations regarding moral living (4:3-8).

THESSALONIANS 2, BOOK OF

Paul's second letter to the saints in Thessalonica was written not long after the first one, while the apostle was still at Corinth (Acts 18:11). This epistle seeks to correct an erroneous impression, entertained by some at Thessalonica, that the Lord's return was imminent. Paul cautions that the Second Coming will not occur until a major apostasy has been manifested – which already was in its beginning phase. The "man of sin" is to be revealed, but Christ will destroy this movement when he returns. The letter exhorts discipline for idle Christians who refuse to stay in step with the instructions of New Testament doctrine.

TIMOTHY 1, BOOK OF

This is Paul's first letter to his convert, Timothy, who was from the city of Lystra (Acts 16:1). It appears to have been written after Paul's release from his initial Roman imprisonment (Acts 28). Timothy was a frequent traveling companion of the apostle's. Paul warns the young evangelist about false teachers that threatened the faith (1:3-7; 19-20; 4:1ff). The letter provides instruction in "sound doctrine" and guides in the selection of elders, who would oversee the work of local churches, and of deacons, who would serve by carrying out special tasks in the congregations (3:1ff).

TIMOTHY 2, BOOK OF

This is Paul's last letter before his execution. It was written during his final Roman imprisonment. The epistle summons Timothy to Paul's side. It is intended to help Timothy understand the events unfolding in the imperial city. It contains the apostle's touching farewell charge to his young companion in the gospel. He urges Timothy to be a good soldier for the Lord. The epistle also warns of the continuing rise of false teachers who would attempt to corrupt the faith of many.

TITHE

In the N.T. (cf. Heb. 7:6, 9), this term derives from the Greek, *dekatos*, meaning "tenth." (a) In the Patriarchal period of history, it appears to have been the practice that godly men gave a tenth of their income to the service of God (Gen. 14:20; 28:22). (b) Under the Mosaic system, tithing was also an integral part of submission to the law of God (Lev. 27:30-33; 2 Chron. 31:5ff; Neh. 10:37ff), though it eventually was largely ignored (cf. Mal. 3:7-12). (c) There is no N.T. command to "tithe," nor is there an example of the early church practicing tithing. Under the new covenant, which is a better regime with better promises (Heb. 8:6), having a better hope (Heb. 7:19), the Christian gives cheerfully (2 Cor. 9:7) and generously (Rom. 12:8) into the church treasury each Sunday (1 Cor. 16:2). See: GIVING.

TITUS, BOOK OF

Titus was a Gentile co-worker of Paul's whom the apostle had left on the island of Crete to "set in order" certain matters and to work toward the ordination of elders within the local congregations. Titus was to build upon an earlier work that Paul had done in this region. It emphasizes that Christians must be "sound" in doctrine, faith, and speech, and that brethren must be diligent to maintain "good works" (four times this phrase is employed). The book also warns of false teachers and urges that those of a sectarian mentality be rejected (3:10).

TONGUES, SPEAKING IN

Literally speaking, the "tongue" is an organ of taste and speech within the mouth. By metaphorical extension, it is used in literature for a human language. In the N.T., the gift of being able to "speak in tongues" was one of the manifestations of the Holy Spirit (Mk. 16:17; 1 Cor. 12:10). There are two major views within the community of "Christendom" relative to the nature of these "tongues." The "Pentecostals," or "Charismatics," contend that the gift of tongues constituted a "heavenly language," a series of unintelligible sounds, unrelated to normal human speech. By way of contrast, the *actual biblical view* is that the gift of a "tongue" was simply the divinely imposed ability to speak in a human language that had not been learned by the ordinary education process. This is demonstrated by the following points: (a) On the day of Pentecost, the phenomenon of "tongues" is identified quite clearly as human "languages" (Acts 2:3-8). (b) The "tongue" gift provided edification (1 Cor. 14:4) and instruction (14:19); mere sounds do not. (c) In a church assembly composed of various nationalities, one was not to use his "tongue" gift before an alien audience unless someone was present who could "interpret" (i.e., translate) (1 Cor. 14:13, 27-28). (d) If one spoke in a "tongue," and others did not understand the language, the speaker would sound like a "barbarian" (1 Cor. 14:11), which term signifies a foreigner, one of a different language (see Acts 28:2). This is another indication that *human languages* are in view. (e) Tongues were to cease with completion of the N.T. canon (1 Cor. 13:8ff). (f) Finally, there is this point. Those who profess to speak in tongues miraculously reveal a woeful inconsistency, in that they must *teach their missionaries* to speak in the "tongues" of those nations they seek to evangelize.

TRADITION

The term "tradition" renders a Greek word that suggests the idea of "instruction that has been handed down." It takes on two senses in Scripture. (a) "Tradition" may be instruction that is *divinely* originated. Paul commended the Corinthians for holding to the "traditions" he had delivered unto them (1 Cor. 11:2; cf. 2 Thes. 2:15). The brethren at Thessalonica were admonished to disfellowship those who refused to follow the apostles' "tradition" (2 Thes. 3:6). (b) "Tradition" can also refer to *human practices* of long-standing. When human tradition virtually becomes an appendix to divine law, the perpetrators of such custom are transgressors, having gone beyond what "is written" (Mt. 15:3; Col. 2:8; 1 Cor. 4:6 ASV; 2 Jn. 9). (c) It is a sinful act to take the law of God and treat it as mere human "tradition." Similarly, it is evil to elevate men's "traditions" to the status of sacred law. The Roman Catholic Church, for example, holds that the "traditions" of the Church, as handed down over the centuries and ratified by certain synods, assume an authority *equal* to the Scriptures. This is a false dogma.

TRANSLATION

"Translation" is the process of bringing the message of the Scriptures from the original languages – Hebrew, Aramaic (O.T.), and Greek (N.T.) – into the various languages and dialects of the nations of the world. Translations vary in quality. Producing a translation from one language to another is not an easy task. The ideal is to render the message of the Bible in the most accurate and understandable way possible. This involves several things. (a) The best textual base possible. See TEXT. Though the King James Version (1611) is still a wonderful translation, its textual base was exceedingly limited compared to later versions (e.g., the American Standard Version - 1901). (b) The translator who believes he is dealing with *God's* words will be more likely to produce a better rendition than the liberal scholar who believes that the biblical documents are mere human productions with flaws common to man. (c) All translations will include, to some degree, the translators' bias with reference to difficult passages, the rendition of which is subject to some controversy. The KJV reflects some Calvinistic influence (cf. Eph. 2:3 – *"by nature* children of wrath"). The RSV's "young woman" (Isa. 7:14) hints of liberal bias. The New World Translation (published by the Watchtower society) is rank with the theological flavor of that cult. (d) The "translation philosophy" of the translator will be a factor in how close the version remains to the original text. While it is not always possible to yield a translation that corresponds to the original text, word-for-word, the closer one is able to stay to the original, the richer the yield will be. The more modern approach, called Dynamic Equivalence (as seen in the NIV and numerous other modern versions) allows more latitude to the translator, hence surrenders itself to a looser version. (e) While not all versions are of equal merit, one could learn how to become a Christian, and arrive in heaven at last, from most any of the modern versions. It must be noted that Jesus and the apostles frequently quoted from the Septuagint, which was considerably inferior to the Hebrew Scriptures. This was because it was the more common Bible of that day. In the modern world of many translations (some of which can be helpful tools), the student today should strive for the utmost accuracy in a day-to-day study Bible. The use of a more conservative version would facilitate this goal.

TRANSUBSTANTIATION

This word signifies "change in substance," and it reflects the Roman Catholic doctrine that in the communion service, when the priest pronounces the words, "this is my body" and "this is my blood," the communion elements (bread and fruit of the vine) turn into the "real presence" of Christ. The dogma is false, having its origin in about A.D. 1215. (a) Jesus' statement, "this is my blood..." (Mt. 26:28) obviously was not a literal affirmation, for he was still alive and his blood was yet in his body. (b) The Lord's comment that the supper would be in "remembrance" of him (Lk. 22:19) clearly indicates that his *literal body* would not be present. (c) The drinking of actual blood would be inconsistent with later apostolic instruction (Acts 15:20, 29). (d) The transformation of the elements would require a miracle, and the days of miracles were terminated with the completion of the N.T. See MIRACLES. The Lutheran idea of "consubstantiation" is equally erroneous. This is the theory that the "real" body and blood of Jesus are *co-mingled* with the actual bread and fruit of the vine while the communion is being observed. There is no evidence, biblical or otherwise, for this notion.

TRINITY

The word "Trinity" does not occur in the Scriptures. The term combines the dual concepts of "three," and "unity," and thus it *does* represent a biblical idea, namely that the Godhead is composed of three distinct *personalities* which share one, identical *essence*, the nature of deity. God is "one" as to essence (Dt. 6:4; Jas. 2:19), but the divine nature is possessed by Father, Son, and Holy Spirit (Mt. 28:19; 2 Cor. 13:14). See GOD.

TRUTH

The term "truth" carries several connotations in the Bible. (a) Truth can convey the idea of *loyalty*. Those who abide in Jesus' teaching are "truly" his disciples (Jn. 8:31). (b) True may denote that which is *genuine*, in contrast to the counterfeit. God is "true" deity; idols are not (1 Thes. 1:9). (c) Truth is that which conforms to *reality*; it stands in opposition to the lie (Rom. 1:25). (d) Truth is that which remains *consistent*. The "sum" of God's word is truth (Psa. 119:160 NASB). (e) Truth is that which is in harmony with a *standard*. The Lord's word is the truth (Jn. 17:17), and by that standard men must worship him (Jn. 4:24). (f) Truth sometimes expresses the idea of *honesty* (Mk. 5:33). (g) In order for "truth" to *avail* a person, it must be known (Jn. 8:32; cf. 1 Tim. 2:4), understood (cf. Eph. 5:17), believed and loved (2 Thes. 2:10-12), and obeyed (Rom. 2:8-9; 1 Jn. 1:6; 2:4). One must strive to "walk" in truth always (2 Jn. 4; 3 Jn. 3), never hinder it (Rom. 1:18), withstand it (2 Tim. 3:8), or turn away from it (Tit. 1:14).

TYPE

A "type" (*tupos*) is a prophetic, pictorial preview, which finds its fulfillment in an "antitype." Types are grounded in historical events, but they are symbolic in import. These forms of figurative "prophecy" are found in the O.T., and they point to Christ and his new covenant regime. Some examples are: (a) The passover lamb was a picture of Christ (Jn. 1:29; 1 Cor. 5:7). (b) Moses, as a great prophet and leader, was a symbol of Jesus (Dt. 18:15ff). (c) Jonah's deliverance from the great fish's body was predictive of the resurrection of Christ (Mt. 12:40-41). (d) The tabernacle (and later the temple) were types of the church and heaven (Heb. 9:1ff; 1 Cor. 3:16). See ANTITYPE.

UNDERSTANDING

Some religions are based upon philosophical premises that are embraced emotionally, apart from intellectual substance. That is not the case with Christianity. Christianity is grounded in history, and there are historical facts and concepts that must be understood and endorsed, preliminary to accessing the blessings of the divine arrangement. One of the fundamental differences between the Mosaic system, and that of the religion established by Jesus, is this: the former incorporated the Hebrews into the covenant arrangement when they were *born*. Males were circumcised at eight days of age as a sign that they were under the covenant. But under the Christian economy, one *first* reaches a state of spiritual and moral responsibility; he then must be exposed to the facts of the gospel, understand and believe them, and, upon that basis, surrender to the truth (cf. Jer. 31:31-34; Mt. 13:14ff; Jn. 6:44-45; Acts 17:11; Eph. 1:18; 5:17). This is why it is so imperative that Christian teachers proclaim the truth accurately, clearly, and without compromise.

UNITY

While the term "unity" is rare in the English Bible (Psa. 133:1; Eph. 4:3; 4:13), the *idea* prevails profusely in a variety of contexts. (a) Unity is that oneness that obtains perfectly among the members of the divine Godhead – Father, Son, and Holy Spirit. These holy Persons are "one" (Dt. 6:4; Jn. 10:30; Jas. 2:19). They share the same essence (combination of divine traits), they are one in purpose, and they function in perfect union in the interest of humanity. (b) There is a unity within the marriage relationship when a man and woman are joined to one another in harmony with the sacred will of God (Gen.

2:24; Mt. 19:5-6). Only death or sexual infidelity can break that unity. (c) In the divine scheme of things, there was to be a unity among all believers in Christ, in terms of faith and practice. Jesus established only "one" church (cf. Mt. 16:18; Jn. 10:16; 11:52; 1 Cor. 12:20; Eph. 2:16; 4:4). The model church was of "one heart and soul" (Acts 4:32). Division is condemned (1 Cor. 1:10ff; Rom. 16:17; Gal. 5:20). Today's multitude of differing denominations reflects a digressive development that was ominously foretold (2 Thes. 2:1ff; 1 Tim. 4:1ff; 2 Tim. 4:1ff), and is contrary to the expressed will of Jesus (Jn. 17:20-21). (d) In Ephesians 4:13, the "unity" of "the faith" (gospel system) most likely refers to the conclusion of the revelatory process by which the "in part" process (cf. 1 Cor. 13:8ff) was brought to fulfillment by the completion of the N.T. canon, which constitutes a unified body of truth. The unity of the biblical documents is a powerful evidence of their divine origin. See CONTRADICTION.

UNIVERSALISM

The false idea that all men will be saved ultimately is called "universalism." (a) Universalism is illogical; it suggests that man's use of his power of choice – for good or evil – is irrelevant. He will be saved no matter what his choices are. (b) It is a reflection upon the justice of God. It asserts that obedience and disobedience will be rewarded equally. (c) The doctrine is totally at variance with the explicit testimony of Scripture (Mt. 7:13-14; Mk. 16:16; 2 Thes. 1:7ff). (d) Universalism is a human illusion based upon what men *wish* was the case, rather than what *is* the case. (e) In 1961 there was a consolidation of the Unitarian and Universalist churches in the United States; there are more than 1,000 of these churches. It is a religion of no substance, with only a shadowy relationship to Christianity.

UNCTION, EXTREME

"Extreme Unction" is one of the so-called "sacraments" of the Roman Catholic Church. It is the action of a priest in applying oil to someone who is at the point of death. The priest reads prayers and grants "absolution" for sins. The candidate need not have any awareness of what is transpiring. There is not the slightest Bible sanction for this practice. Only two cases of anointing with oil are mentioned in the N.T. One was in connection with the performance of miracles (Mk. 6:13), the second had to do with calling the elders to pray for the sick with a view to *healing* – not dying (Jas. 5:14-15), which very likely had to do with supernatural intervention as well. Moreover, it is wholly erroneous to suggest that forgiveness of sins could be granted to an unconscious person who has neither the inclination nor ability to respond to the will of God in obtaining pardon.

VERSIONS, BIBLE

A version is a translation of the Scriptures from the original languages (Hebrew, Aramaic, and Greek) into another language. Versions may be classified as ancient or modern. (a) Some ancient versions are noteworthy. The *Septuagint* (represented by the Roman numerals LXX) is a Greek translation of the O.T. that dates from the third century before Christ; it was produced by Jews in Alexandria. It contains significant variations from the Hebrew text. Esther is much longer in the LXX, while Job is about one-fourth shorter. It also contained apocryphal books. The LXX was, however, the common Bible for the man-on-the-street in the days of Christ, and it was used by Jesus and the apostles in their teaching endeavors. The *Syriac* version of the O.T. dates from the mid-second/early third century A.D.; it omits the apocryphal books. The *Syriac* version of the N.T. dates from the mid-to-late fifth century A.D., and resulted in the widespread distribution of the Scriptures. The *Ethiopic* version (fourth century) facilitated the spread of the Scriptures in Africa. The *Gothic* version (fourth century) propagated the Bible in Germany. The *Latin Vulgate* (fourth century) became the official version of the Roman Catholic Church. In the ninth century, *Arabic* versions were produced in an attempt to negate the spreading influence of Islam. (b) For our purposes, modern versions date from the time of the *King James Version* (1611). The *English Revised Version* came in 1881, and its American cousin, the *American Standard Version*, arrived in 1901. Each of these was a faithful attempt to reproduce the original texts as accurately as possible. The *Revised Standard Version* (1946/52) was also a fairly literal translation, but its translators were theologically liberal and that inclination shows at times (cf. Isa. 7:14). The *New English Bible* (1970) charted new territory. It was a "looser" rendition of the original text, attempting to bring "thoughts" across, rather than "words." The *New International Version* (1973/78) admitted that it did not attempt a word-for-word rendition; it adopts the "Dynamic Equivalence" procedure. Both the *New American Standard Bible* (1963/70/97) and the *New King James Version* (1979/82) attempt a literal translation and are reliable versions, though the NASB has the better textual base. The *English Standard Version* (2001) appears to be a strong translation with a literal rendition is most instances. See TRANSLATION.

VIRGIN BIRTH OF CHRIST

The doctrine of the virgin birth of Jesus is one of the lines of evidence establishing the Lord's identity as the Son of God. The angel Gabriel said to Mary, a "virgin" (Lk. 1:27): "The holy thing which is begotten shall be called the Son of God" (1:35). Proofs for the historicity of the virgin birth are as follows: (a) It was prophesied by Isaiah seven centuries before the birth of Jesus (Isa. 7:14; Mt. 1:22-23). (b) The virgin-birth event was affirmed by the apostle Matthew. In his legal genealogy of Christ, the apostle employs "begat" thirty-nine times; the term is omitted as a connective to Jesus (1:16). The pronoun "whom" (v. 16) is feminine, singular, thus excluding Joseph. Mary was with child before she and Joseph "came together" (v. 18). The conception was by the Spirit's power, i.e., miraculous (vv. 18, 20). Initially, Joseph was inclined to divorce Mary, which indicates he was not the father of the child (v. 19). Joseph was never intimate with Mary until *after* the Savior's birth (v. 25). (c) Luke, a physician (Col. 4:14), affirmed the doctrine of the virgin birth (Lk. 1:26ff). A doctor is the last person who would be convinced of such a phenomenon – unless there was compelling evidence. And Luke had carefully investigated matters concerning Jesus (Lk. 1:1-4). (d) If Mary knew that Jesus had an *earthly* father, would she have stood at the foot of the cross (Jn. 19:26) and watched her son being murdered for the *claim* of being the "Son of the blessed One" (Mk. 14:62)? Such a conclusion would make Mary one of the vilest characters of feminine history. The biblical teaching of the virgin birth is not the only proof that Jesus is the Son of God, but it is an important plank in the platform.

WALK

The common word for "walk" in the N.T. is *peripateo*. It means to walk around, or, in a figurative sense, "to conduct oneself" in a certain way. The topic is approached both negatively and positively in the Scriptures. (a) The Christian is not to walk after the common "manner" that men ordinarily do, i.e., disregarding the will of God (1 Cor. 3:3). We are not to walk in pursuit of the desires of the flesh (Rom. 8:4), nor in a crafty, dishonest fashion (2 Cor. 4:2). God's child must not walk after the vanity of his mind (Eph. 4:17), nor by sight (2 Cor. 5:7). And those who walk disorderly are worthy of discipline (2 Thes. 3:6). (b) On the other hand, we are admonished to walk in newness of life (Rom. 6:4), following the instruction of the Spirit through the Scriptures (Rom. 8:4; Eph. 6:17). We walk by faith (2 Cor. 5:7), in love (Eph. 5:2), in honesty (Rom. 13:13), and in truth (2 Jn. 4). We must strive to walk in wisdom (Col. 4:5), pursuing the commandments of the Lord (2 Jn. 4:6), while exhibiting good works (Eph. 2:10).

WAR

Two principal Greek words are employed in the N.T. to represent the idea of "fighting" and "war." *Polemeo* (18 times) means to "fight" or "make war." *Strateuomai* (7 times) is to "carry out a military engagement, to be a soldier." "War" is used in both literal and figurative senses in the Scriptures. (a) *Physical* warfare is referred to on occasion (see Mt. 24:6; Lk. 14:31), and is called "carnal" or "of the flesh" (2 Cor. 10:4 ASV). There is no sanction in the N.T. for Christians to be engaged in such conflicts. Opposite admonitions are the rule (Mt. 5:9; 43ff; 26:52; Jn. 18:36; Rom. 12:17ff; 2 Cor. 10:4ff; Eph. 6:12; Heb. 12:14). If the Christian loves his brother (1 Pet. 1:22), his neighbor (Mt.

22:39), and his enemy (Mt. 5:43ff), with whom shall he war? (b) There is a *spiritual* warfare between the forces of good and evil. Christians are to "war *the good* warfare" (1 Tim. 1:18; cf. 2 Tim. 4:7), arming themselves with *spiritual* weapons (Eph. 6:11ff), bringing the "thoughts" of men into captivity (2 Cor. 10:5). (c) There is the *internal* "war" against sin that rages in every Christian's soul as he attempts to defeat the flesh in deference to spiritual values (Rom. 7:23; Jas. 4:1; 1 Pet. 2:11).

WAY

A number of terms, both in the O.T. and the N.T., suggest the idea of a "path" or "way" of travel. The words come to be employed of a "course of conduct," whether for good (Ex. 18:20; 32:8; Dt. 31:29; Jer. 6:16) or evil (Num. 22:32; Psa. 139:24; Isa. 65:2; Acts 14:16). (a) Jesus declared that he is "the way" to the Father (Jn. 14:6), and that all others who attempt to provide a way are "thieves and robbers" (Jn. 10:8). In none other besides Jesus Christ is salvation to be found (Acts 4:11-12). (b) The kingdom of the Lord Jesus is designated as "the way" no less than six times in the book of Acts (9:2; 19:9, 23; 22:4; 24:4, 22). The "way" of true Christianity excludes other religious systems because they are not authorized by the Lord.

WILL OF GOD

Jesus once urged that the "will" of God might be done on earth, just as it is in heaven (Mt. 6:10). Jehovah's will is that which is best for humanity, and which he requires that we implement in our lives. The Lord has the "right" to exert his will because of *who he is* (deity), and he has the "ability" to impose his will in any way that is consistent with the sum of his attributes. The "will of God" is expressed in a variety of ways. (a) There is the *ideal* will of God. He would like for all people to be saved (2 Pet. 3:9), but he will not rob them of their power of choice and force redemption upon them. (b) The *permissive* will of God relates to the fact that the Lord allows men to reap the evil consequences of their rebellion so that they may taste the fruit of their folly (Mt. 19:8; Acts 14:16). (c) Jehovah's will was *directly* implemented in the first century in the performance of miracles, in order to authenticate the divine revelation being given from heaven (Acts 3:1-10; 4:16). (d) The *indirect* will of God is orchestrated by means of providential activity, i.e., God working behind the scenes to accomplish his purposes (Gen. 45:7-8; 50:20). (e) The *objective* will of God has been made known through the revelation of Scripture. This "will" may be known (Col. 1:9), tested (Rom. 12:2), and understood (Eph. 5:17). It is a part of a teaching system (Jn. 7:17), which must be obeyed (Mt. 7:21), and not rejected (Lk. 7:30). (f) The *implied* will of God is that which can be deduced logically by the proper use of one's reasoning faculties. Paul "concluded" that it was God's will that he preach in Macedonia – as a result of a supernatural vision he saw in the night at Troas (Acts 16:10). The Creator wants man to *know* and to *obey* his revealed will.

WINE

A number of Hebrew words are rendered by the English "wine," the most common of which are *yayin* (134 times) and *tirosh* (33 times). The basic term for "wine" in the Greek N.T. is *oinos* (33 times). (a) "Wine" can be a generic term, occasionally referring to fresh grape juice. Isaiah referred to "wine in the presses" (16:10), which obviously is simply the juice of the grape. There were ways in antiquity to preserve juice all year long from fermentation. There is no reason to assume that the "wine" made by Jesus was alcoholic in content (Jn. 2:1ff). (b) Frequently, "wine" refers to a beverage capable of producing intoxication (Eph. 5:18). There are, therefore, many warnings against the indiscriminate use of wine (Prov. 20:1; 21:17; 23: 20-21; 30-31; Isa. 5:22; 28:7; Joel 1:5; Amos 6:6; Hab. 2:5; 1 Tim. 3:8; Tit. 2:3). See DRUNKENESS. (c) Wine is sometimes viewed as a substance of medicinal value (Lk. 10:34; 1 Tim. 5:8). (d) The term also may be employed as a symbol of the wrath of God (Jer. 25:15; 51:7; Rev. 14:10; 16:19).

WOMAN

Woman was fashioned from flesh and bone taken from the side of man (Gen. 2:21-24). Male and female qualities were designed by God (Mt. 19:4); these characteristics are not accidental developments of an imagined "evolutionary" process. The Hebrew term for "woman" is *ishsha*, thought to derive from a root signifying "soft, delicate," hinting, perhaps of her "God-given gifts and sensitivities" in contributing to the emotional needs of humanity. (a) In male/female relationships, man has been appointed the role of "head" over the woman (Gen. 2:18, 20; 3:16; 1 Cor. 11:7-9; Eph. 5:22ff; 1 Tim. 2:11-12), and this limits female activity in certain environments (1 Cor. 14:34; 1 Tim. 2:8, 12ff). This relationship must not be abused by man. (b) God greatly honored womankind by sending the Savior into the world by means of a woman (Lk. 1:42; Gal. 4:4; cf. 1 Tim. 2:15). In the first-century environment women were valuable assets in the service of God by means of their prayers (Acts 1:14), their good works and almsdeeds (Acts 9:36), and in providing hospitality (Acts 12:12; 16:14; 1 Tim. 5:10). In harmony with their divinely prescribed roles, women taught the gospel (Acts 18:26; 21:9; Tit. 2:3-4). They functioned as godly wives (Acts 18:2) and mothers (2 Tim. 1:5; 3:14-15), contributing greatly to the growth – internally and externally – of the church of Jesus Christ.

WORKS

The term "works" is a perfectly noble word; yet, in the minds of some, there is a distorted view of this biblical term. Especially has the Protestant world reacted negatively to Catholicism's "works system" – an ideology contrary to the divine plan of redemption. This reaction, however, is itself an extreme, equally as dangerous as Catholic dogma. Note some of the various categories of works: (a) There are the works of divine creation which bring glory to the Creator (Psa. 19:1-3; Rom. 1: 20; Heb. 1:10; 2:7). (b) There were miraculous works by which God authenticated revelatory messages through his specially appointed spokesmen (Acts 2:22). (c) The law of Moses was characterized by works. These were works, however, through which there was no justification (Rom. 3:28), because no one could keep perfectly that law – hence all under the system were "cursed" by it (Gal. 3:10-11). Christ was absolutely essential as a sacrifice for those who lived under Mosaic law (Gal. 4:4; Heb. 9:15-17). (d) There are works of human "merit" which, though perhaps benevolent in motive and effect, cannot save a person (Eph. 2:8-9; 2 Tim. 1:9; Tit. 3:5). A good work *per se* has no intrinsic power to cancel sin. (e) Actions implemented in response to commands of God are also called "works" (Eph. 3:10; Tit. 3:8; Rev. 2:26). Faith is a work (Jn. 6:27-29; 1 Thes. 1:3; 2 Thes. 1:11; Jas. 2:14ff), and so is repentance (Mt. 12: 41; Jonah 3:10). Baptism is a work only in the sense that it expresses obedience to a divine command (Acts 2:38; 10:48).

Baptism is called the "washing of regeneration," and it is distinguished from "works" of human "righteousness" (Tit. 3:5). (f) At the day of Judgment, men will be judged by their earthly works (2 Cor. 11:15; Rev. 20:12-13; 22:12).

WORSHIP

References to "worship" are common in both the O.T. and the N.T. The Hebrew term *shachah* (about 100 times) refers to "bowing" before an object of religious devotion. Similarly, *proskuneo* (59 times) in the N.T. means to prostrate oneself, do obeisance. Worship can be offered to the true God (Gen. 22:1-5), or it may be vainly rendered to a false god (Ex. 20:4-6; 2 Kgs. 10:19). In order for worship to be acceptable, several divine criteria must be satisfied. (a) Worship must be submitted to deity alone (Mt. 4:10); neither angels (Rev. 19:10) nor ordinary men (Acts 10:25-26) are worthy of worship. Because God is a "spirit" being (Jn. 4:24), humans are not permitted to worship him by the use of material objects, e.g., images (Dt. 4:12; 15-18). The fact that Christ was worshipped, and that he accepted such adoration, is an unanswerable argument for his deity (Mt. 8:2; 9:18; 14:33). (b) Worship to God must be rendered with utmost sincerity (Josh. 24:14; Jn. 4:24), not hypocritically (Mt. 15:7-9), for the purpose of show (Mt. 6:1ff), or arrogantly (Lk. 18:10ff). (c) Worship must follow a prescribed procedure, that of "truth" (Jn. 4:24), which means in accordance with God's word (Jn. 17:17). Ignorant worship will not be accepted (Acts 17:23). On the Lord's day, Christians worship by observing the Lord's supper (Acts 20:7; 1 Cor. 11:20ff), singing (Eph. 5:19; Col. 3:16), praying (Acts 2:42; 1 Cor. 14:15), teaching the gospel (Acts 2:42; Rom. 15:16), and contributing from their weekly incomes (1 Cor. 16:2).

ZECHARIAH, BOOK OF

Zechariah was a companion prophet with Haggai. The latter sternly admonished the Hebrews to rid themselves of self-interest and to complete work on the temple in the post-Babylonian captivicx here is a tremendous emphasis on the blessings associated with the promise of the coming Messiah, who would serve simultaneously as both a king and a priest in the new age, i.e., the Christian dispensation (6:12-13). The book is characterized by several symbolic visions.

ZEPHANIAH, BOOK OF

The prophet Zephaniah was the great, great grandson of king Hezekiah (1:1). His prophetic ministry was conducted in the days of Judah's good king, Josiah (cir. 639-09 B.C.). Josiah came to the throne as a boy of eight, but he grew spiritually (2 Kg. 22, 23; 2 Chron. 34, 35), and initiated a great reform when a copy of "the law" was found in the temple in the eighteenth year of his reign. The prophet foretells the coming "great day of Jehovah" that was hastening and near (1:14) – an allusion to the impending Babylonian captivity. Other evil nations would also see the wrath of God. But there was hope in the promise of the coming Messianic age (cf. 3:8ff).

SOURCES

Balz, Horst & Schneider, Gerhard (1991), *Exegetical Dictionary of the New Testament* (Grand Rapids: Eerdmans), Three Volumes.

Blaiklock, E.M. (1970), *The Archaeology of the New Testament* (Grand Rapids: Zondervan).

Cross, Frank L., Ed. (1958), *The Oxford Dictionary of the Christian Church* (London: Oxford University Press).

Danker, F.W., Baur, W., Arndt, W.F., Gingrich, F.W. (2000), *A Greek-English Lexicon of the New Testament and Other Early Christian Literature* (Chicago: University of Chicago).

Douglas, J.D., Ed. (1962), *The New Bible Dictionary* (Grand Rapids: Eerdmans).

Earl, Ralph (2000), *Word Meanings in the New Testament* (Peabody, MA: Hendrickson).

Ferm, Vergilius (1945), *An Encyclopedia of Religion* (New York: Philosophical Library).

Foster, R.C. (1971), *Studies in the Life of Christ* (Grand Rapids: Baker).

Harrison, E.F., Bromiley, G.W. & Henry, Carl (1999), *Wycliffe Dictionary of Theology* (Peabody, MA: Hendrickson).

Harvey, Van A. (1964), *A Handbook of Theological Terms* (New York: Macmillan).

Horn, Siegfried H. (1960), *The Seventh-day Adventist Bible Dictionary* (Washington, D.C.: Review & Herald).

Luck, G. Coleman (1955), *The Bible Book By Book – An Introduction to Bible Synthesis* (Chicago: Moody).

Pfeiffer, C.F., Vos, H.F., Rea, J. (1998), *Wycliffe Bible Dictionary* (Peabody, MA: Hendrickson).

Thayer, J.H. (1959), *A Greek-English Lexicon of the New Testament* (Edinburgh: T.&T. Clark).

Trench, R.C. (1890), *New Testament Synonyms* (London: Kegan Paul, Trench, Trubner & Co.).

Vine, W.E. (1991), *Amplified Expository Dictionary of New Testament Words* (Iowa Falls, IA: World).

Wilson, Robert Dick (1929), *A Scientific Investigation of the Old Testament* (New York: Harper & Bros.).

The Bible & Science

by Wayne Jackson

Have the discoveries of modern science rendered the Scriptures obsolete? May one assert that the "spiritual" truths of the Bible are meaningful, but its "scientific" references are flawed?

No, that is not consistent. The "sum" of the various parts of Sacred Writ are "truth" (Psa. 119:160 ASV). The Scriptures are scientifically credible. In fact, "science" never quite "catches up" with Scripture.

The book is comprised of thirteen chapters. Questions at the end of each chapter stimulate deeper reflection, making this book ideal for the classroom.

Order your copy today:

Courier Publications
7809 N. Pershing Ave.
Stockton, CA 95207

http://www.courierpublications.com.